T0031910

Selling in the Real World®
2nd Edition

Selling in the Real World®

WHY EVERYTHING'S CHANGED
WHY NOTHING'S CHANGED

by LARRY STERNLIEB

NEW YORK

LONDON · NASHVILLE · MELBOURNE · VANCOUVER

Selling in the Real World 2nd Edition

WHY EVERYTHING'S CHANGED, WHY NOTHING'S CHANGED

© 2023 Larry Sternlieb

All rights reserved. No portion of this book may be reproduced, stored in a retrieval system, or transmitted in any form or by any means—electronic, mechanical, photocopy, recording, scanning, or other—except for brief quotations in critical reviews or articles, without the prior written permission of the publisher.

Published in New York, New York, by Morgan James Publishing. Morgan James is a trademark of Morgan James, LLC. www.MorganJamesPublishing.com

Proudly distributed by Ingram Publisher Services.

A **FREE** ebook edition is available for you or a friend with the purchase of this print book.

CLEARLY SIGN YOUR NAME ABOVE

Instructions to claim your free ebook edition:
1. Visit MorganJamesBOGO.com
2. Sign your name CLEARLY in the space above
3. Complete the form and submit a photo of this entire page
4. You or your friend can download the ebook to your preferred device

ISBN 9781636980768 paperback
ISBN 9781636980775 ebook
Library of Congress Control Number: 2022948089

Cover and Interior Design by:
Randy Martin
martinDESIGN.info

Morgan James is a proud partner of Habitat for Humanity Peninsula and Greater Williamsburg. Partners in building since 2006.

Get involved today! Visit: www.morgan-james-publishing.com/giving-back

DEDICATION

In memory of my parents, Max & Mollie,
In honor of my sister, Myra,
And also Patricia.

table of contents

introduction

SALES IS AN ART FORM. We use it to get a raise, to get a date, or even to get a high-level executive to agree to a twenty-million dollar order. Sales is used by all of us, whether we are aware of using it or not. We use it all the time. The better you are at sales, the better your results.

If sales is an art form, is it also a science? Can those of us who were not born with a silver tongue learn to sell better? Are there strategies that will make someone more skillful at the art of selling? Do you think a person born with the natural ability to draw can improve how well they draw? The answer is: of course.

This book, *Selling in the Real World*, is filled with plans, behaviors, and attitudes; principles that will improve your ability to sell. It is not simply lists of tricks to pull. These are well-proven principles that will help you create an easy to understand track to run on. And a better track always produces better results — results that are easier, faster, and unbeatable.

Selling in the Real World is not a feel-good book. It was designed to be hard-hitting, to provide a solid track for both the experienced sales professional looking to refocus and polish their skills, as well as for those about to create their livelihood from the art of Sales for the first time.

For many of the situations in this book, I've created dialogs between a person named Larry and a person called Mr. O'Conner. You may find some of the dialogue to be too formal for your taste. Because of the wide variety in regional differences and variations in speech patterns, I intentionally created them that way. I strongly encourage you not to use my words exactly. Get the sense of what I'm saying, and then put it in your own words. Using someone else's words, no matter how well written, often sounds fake. Be yourself. Use the words you're comfortable with.

And KIS: Keep it Simple. Don't try to say any more than you need to. Let the customers do the talking; you supply the answers to their problems. That's the secret of selling — solving their problems.

I remember vividly when I first started in sales for Xerox. I was twenty-five years old, my parents had passed away when I was nineteen, I had just resigned from a management position with the State of Ohio, and I had no savings. So I knew that whatever I accomplished on my first day out in the field was going to impact the rest of my life This was my first solo sales call. I was driving around the block over and over again, trying to get up the nerve to get out of my car and walk through the door. Making this sales call was a necessity, failure was not an option. Essentially, I had no one to turn to but myself. So I gutted it up, parked my car, and went in to the very first sales call of my life.

That day, I went on to make more than thirty face-to-face, cold calls and set up several more future sales. Looking back, that sounds a whole lot easier than it really was.

What I discovered was the beginning of the mind-set I would use throughout my career to become — and remain — successful. I survived through hard work and an engaging personality that drew in customers and turned them into buyers. I was always positive and assumed the sale. I made sure I knew my product perfectly, as well as my competitors' products. I decided I wanted to survive in sales, learned not to give up on a sale, and discovered how to ignite the fire to find new opportunities. Most importantly, I taught myself to win. And then, I did it all again. Every day.

To be honest, there were many times in my lengthy career when I allowed myself to weaken and feel sorry. It was my misfortune that both my parents became sick and died when I was nineteen. It wasn't the way I wanted or dreamed my life would be. I told myself that anyone living with what I had to live with had the right to allow negativity to creep in. I wondered, "Why me? Why wasn't I blessed with inheriting a lot of money?"

But I knew that focusing on the negative wasn't useful and that thinking and living as if it were wasn't going to pay the rent. So, I taught myself to be my greatest supporter. I decided that the cards life had dealt me were not going to determine how I had to live. They were simply the cards I was dealt and I had to play them. Or fold.

I had no time to dwell on the negative. I had to be positive and push myself to work as hard as possible. I knew that this was more than a job.

This was first about survival and then about success. It's true that I didn't plan to be a salesman. But after choosing this profession — which by the way can generate the greatest income outside of medicine or law — I was determined to succeed — no matter what.

My message to you, the reader of *Selling in the Real World* is this. If you want to be successful at Sales, you can do it. If you want to make money, you will. If you want to live a good life, you can. If you want to help others be successful in their business and life, then you have come to the right place. This is the successful attitude I encourage you to embrace:

- *Selling in the Real World* is a person-to-person experience.
- People buy from people.
- Understand your customers and their issues.
- Listen carefully to their requirements.
- Treat them like a friend.
- Help them succeed.

You may think today is a different time, and that what worked ages ago is no longer valuable. If that's what you think, you are mistaken. We, people, are the same as we've always been. Our essence, our core has not changed. What changes are the products and the technologies with which we live. Technology always advances; Sales techniques that are successful, however, rarely change much at all.

I am pleased to be able to share my more than forty years of corporate sales experience, as well as the knowledge I've gained from the advanced courses I have both taken and facilitated. I hope you will be able to enjoy the pleasure of a satisfying career in sales as I have.

What you have in your hands, *Selling in the Real World*, is a process that's proven. It's a process that works. Take advantage of it!
I did. And I'm telling you it works. It may not always be easy, but it will always be as successful as you want it to be. Work hard. Life pays you back based on what you put into it.

I put everything into Sales that I could. And I got back more than I expected. I know you can, too.

The only thing you need to be successful in sales is the willingness to do everything in your power to succeed.

The choice is yours.

chapter one

The Psychology of Selling

PSYCHOLOGY

Every job has downsides. The downsides of sales include
- Living with rejection,
- Losing opportunities in which you did everything right to obtain the business but still didn't,
- Dealing with a wide range of psyches and behaviors of clients and coworkers
- Physical and mental strain
- Internal politics that can work against you

To overcome the downsides, successful sales professionals learn:
- To be their own best friend and biggest supporter
- To be a firm realist
- What to do and what not to do
- What to think and what not to think
- How to behave and how not to behave

And then there are what I call the Essences of Success:
- A positive attitude
- The willingness to work hard at all times
- The ability to instill confidence

LET'S START WITH A POSITIVE ATTITUDE

Things are neither good nor bad. They are what we make them. Being good or bad is the result of choice — and most often that choice is ours. One of the crucial facts of life is this: our mind and our thoughts are responsible for 90 percent of our success. Therefore, positive thinking is the starting point for you to become successful in sales and ultimately for determining the quality of your life.

Our mind is the most powerful tool we have. It is responsible for each of us being happy or sad, content or dissatisfied, determined or indecisive, strong or weak, positive or negative. The way in which our mind works, therefore, determines the way in which we feel and the way in which we act.

> *"But the world of human behavior is one of the few areas that continue to operate from outmoded theories and information. Many of us are still using a nineteenth-century model of how the brain works and how we behave. We put a label called depression on something, and guess what? We're depressed. The truth is, those terms can be self-fulfilling prophecies."*
> — Anthony Robbins

It is up to us to utilize and harness our energy in a positive manner. If we think positive thoughts, we will behave positively. If we think negative thoughts, we will behave negatively. I know that sounds simple, and I have to admit that early on in my life I thought that. But eventually, I learned it is true — regardless of what I thought. In fact, it is a Universal Truth: the way you think determines the way you act.

....

THE TRAP OF NEGATIVISM

Unfortunately, it is extremely easy to fall into the trap of negativism. Negativism is simply the first step toward depression, a disease that will shut down even the strongest. Clearly, it is important to prevent negativism before it starts. You are the ONLY one who is able to determine the quality of your life. What you think is what you get.

Zig Ziglar talks about overcoming negativism like this:

> *"We believe that this is 'the end', or at least the beginning of the end of negative thinking, negative action and negative reaction; the end of defeatism and despondency; the end of settling for less than you deserve to have and are capable of obtaining; the end of being influenced by little people, with little minds thinking little thoughts about the trivia that is the stock and trade of Mr. & Mrs. Mediocrity. In short, it is the end for you of the world's most deadly disease—'Hardening of the Attitudes.'*

— Zig Ziglar
'Welcome to the Richer Life."

The people, places, and circumstances you encounter as a sales professional will constantly affect you — either positively or negatively. Critical people, politics, cliques of people who choose to exclude you, and small-minded people creating traps, all produce negativism. To avoid their pessimism, you must ignore them and focus on yourself, your goals, and your desired success. The only control you have in life is over yourself; you have no control over others. Choose the attitude you wish to have. Think positive.

Additionally, avoid criticizing others. That's a dark alley you don't want to walk down. When you criticize, you open the path for your brain to accept criticism's negativity and that allows your brain to apply that negativity to you and your opinion of you. I like to think of this as the weight lifter's rule: "That which you focus on gets stronger."

> *"Criticism is futile because it puts a person on the defensive and usually makes him strive to justify himself. Criticism is dangerous because it wounds a person's pride, hurts his sense of importance and arouses resentment."*
> — Dale Carnegie

A word of warning. If you think that people will never know if you criticize or simply talk about them in the office, you are mistaken. People listen and people will always talk. Avoid saying anything about someone you wouldn't say to their face. And if you would be willing to say it to their face, do them the courtesy of saying it to their face.

Most likely, however, the best course of action is to say nothing critical about anyone to anyone. Ever. Focus your time and energy on your own success, not on other people.

THE WILLINGNESS TO WORK HARD AT ALL TIMES

Even when things are going well, sales is tough work. When things are going bad, life seems nearly impossible. In order to thrive and succeed, the Sales Professional must be committed to working hard—at all times. Whether or not you feel like it!

Tom Hanks, in the role of the team manager in A Field of Their Own, has one of the most memorable and useful lines of any movie. He says, "If it were easy, anyone could do it." That applies to baseball, sales, and all aspects of life. Sales is not easy. Not everyone can be a salesperson. Even fewer can be a successful sales person. And no one can be a successful sales professional without the willingness to work hard at all times. **The choice is yours. Make it now.**

THE WILLINGNESS TO WORK HARD

For some, the willingness to work hard is an inherent attitude — they were born with it. It is simply how they attack everything they do. For most of us, however, it is an attitude we must choose to have. Much like we choose to have a positive attitude, we choose to work hard. At all times. At all costs. Whether or not we feel like it. Without this behavior, it is not possible to be a successful sales person. If you do not choose to work hard at all times, do us both a favor: close this book, give it to someone who will work hard, and find something else to do with your life. Without the willingness to work hard, you will not be able to practice the Psychology of Selling, you will not be a salesperson. And you will not be successful.

THE ABILITY TO INSTILL CONFIDENCE

If a salesperson cannot instill confidence, they cannot make a sale; they cannot develop a customer. Without confidence, there is no success. To succeed, you must expect to succeed, every time, all the time. Rain or shine. Good hair days or bad. Confidence is that internal feeling we have that can be felt by those around us. If we are not confident, they know. We can't fake it. Confidence is an automatic response to the problems and circumstances of life.

That doesn't mean it can't be learned. In fact, the opposite is true. Confidence can *only* be learned.

Those who appear to be confident without having the support of knowledge and experience are either arrogant or ignorant. They will be able to get only as far as their customers let them.

Confidence comes from the knowledge that you can perform. Performing comes from overcoming the mistakes you made when you started. Therefore, confidence is the direct result of failure. To be confident, you first must experience failure and then analyze that failure so that you can overcome and prevent that failure in the future. This self-created process generates and strengthens your ability to overcome any problem and thus circumvent failure in the future. Success, then, only comes from failure.

When you have failed and learned to overcome and prevent that failure in the future, you will become confident. When you are confident, you will be successful.

If you want to be successful, get started immediately and don't worry about failing. If and when you fail, analyze your failure, develop systems and techniques to prevent or overcome those situations in the future, and trust your constantly expanding confidence. This is how I learned. This is how I became a confident and successful Sales Professional.

For generations, this process was simply called paying your dues. But Selling in the Real World is a system that expands and builds on that. In addition to the unintentional acquisition of knowledge you accumulate from analyzing your failures, paying your dues includes the intentional acquisition of knowledge: learning your product, knowing your competition, knowing your customer, and searching for new business opportunities.

The ability to instill confidence increases as you learn to face your fears. Don't be afraid to throw a saddle on a horse and jump on for a wild ride. The fear of actually getting on a horse is always worse than riding the horse. And after you get the hang of it; which comes from repetition, analyzing, and internalizing knowledge; riding can be enjoyable. This is very similar to a sales environment in which that wild ride of ups and downs can, in the end, become profitable.

SELLING IS LIKE WARFARE

> *"He will win who, prepared himself, waits to take the enemy unprepared. He will win who has military capacity and is not interfered with by the sovereign. If you know the enemy and know yourself, you need not fear the results of a hundred battles. If you know yourself but not the enemy, for every victory gained you will also suffer a defeat. If you know neither the enemy nor yourself, you will succumb in every battle."* — Sun Tzu

When young people join the military, they must be thoroughly trained and prepared to fight their enemy. Prior to engagement, there can be no fear, only anxiety. Sales can be viewed in the same way and enacted like military warfare. Sales can get ugly, especially if you are not prepared. Not being prepared for your client or your competition and not being able to overcome your own shortcomings and expand your strengths will spell certain defeat.

A Sales Professional, to be completely successfully, must be prepared. When you are prepared, you expect to win. You never doubt your abilities. You know you are the best there is. You do not fear any mission. When you plan, prepare, and know your competition, product, and your clients, you will win your opportunities.

A wining plan includes a highly active schedule full of face-to-face meetings with the Very Important People in your clients' companies. You will stand in front of them and tell them with confidence that they will greatly benefit from your products — and especially from you. You will enjoy being in the spotlight, but never, ever waste anyone's time, especially the time of a major decision-maker.

THINK SUCCESS, NOT FAILURE

> *"In your home, substitute success thinking for failure thinking. When you face a difficult situation think, 'I will win', not 'I'll probably lose.' When you compete with someone else think, 'I'm equal to the best', not 'I'm outclassed.' Let the master thought 'I will succeed' dominate your thinking process. Thinking success conditions your mind to create plans that produce success. Thinking failure does the exact opposite. Failure thinking conditions the mind to think oth-*

er thoughts that produce failure. Remind yourself regularly that you are better than you think you are. Successful people are not supermen. Success does not require a super-intellect. Nor is there anything mystical about success. And success isn't based on luck.

Successful people are just ordinary folks who have developed belief in themselves and what they do. Never—yes, never—sell yourself short. Believe big. The size of your success is determined by the size of your belief. Think little goals and expect little achievements. Think big goals and win big success. Remember this, too! Big ideas and big plans are often easier-certainly no more difficult-than small ideas and small plans."

— David J. Schwartz

Be aware that while many people intend to be successful in sales, only 20 percent are truly successful — those who produce 80 percent of their company's sales revenues. Corporations such as General Electric (for whom I was once employed) had a philosophy that tried to eliminate the bottom twenty percent of their sales force every year and reload with newly hired sales people, introducing new hungry, blood into their sales organization.

The question is: Why do the top twenty percent succeed and the bottom twenty fail?

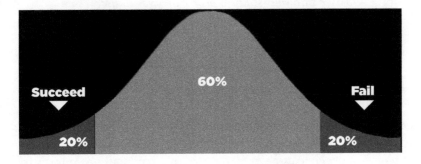

There are contributing circumstances, such as being in the wrong place at the wrong time — I know this happens, first hand. But the following three areas are the prime contributors to one's success or failure in sales:

> Fear
> Excuses
> Procrastination

FEAR

> *"So, first of all, let me assert my firm belief that the only thing we have to fear is...fear itself — nameless, unreasoning, unjustified terror which paralyzes needed efforts to convert retreat into advance."*
> — Franklin Delano Roosevelt,
>   32nd President of The United States of America

Fear is the inability to visualize ourselves winning. We are afraid we will not be successful. We say and/or believe things such as: "I'm not one of the chosen people. I can't charm them. I don't have a great personality. I'm not attractive enough. Nothing goes right for me. I'll never get this large sale. My competition is too great. I'll never make any money. Woe is me."

This mindset takes a person down faster than a large cement block attached to the ankle as they enter a body of water. Either play to win or don't play at all. Never sabotage yourself with negative thoughts. Don't be afraid of anything except of being afraid.

The cure for fear is a positive attitude.

EXCUSES

> *"Go deep into your study of people and you'll discover unsuccessful people suffer a mind deadening thought disease. We call this disease excusitis. Every failure has this disease in its advanced form. And most 'average' persons have at least a mild case of it."*
> — David J. Schwartz

Don't make excuses. About anything. No matter how good or bad your current situation, it is your reality at that exact moment. You don't lose a deal because you had a cold or a hangnail on your big toe. Any loss you experience lands squarely on your own shoulders. If you fail, it is no one's fault except yours.

Think about and consider losses simply as your process of learning to get better.

Don't make excuses. No one will respect you, especially the person who matters the most — you!

The cure for making excuses is to accept responsibility for your actions. All of them.

PROCRASTINATION

> "*Hoping, Wishing, and Maybe, three neurotic phases of the procrastinator make up the support system for maintaining put-it-off behavior.*
>
> *'I hope things will work out.'*
> *'I wish things were better.'*
> *'Maybe it'll be okay.'*
>
> *There you have the deferrer's delight. As long as you say maybe or hope or wish, you can use these as rationale for not doing anything now. All wishing and hoping are a waste of time – the folly of fairyland residents. No amount of either ever got accomplished. They are merely convenient escape clauses from rolling up your sleeves on the tasks that you've decided are important enough to be on your list of life activities.*"
> — Dr. Wayne W. Dyer

Don't procrastinate. Procrastination is perhaps the darkest alley for any Sales Professional. The cure for procrastination is the same as Nike's slogan: "Just Do It!"

SOME FINAL POINTS

• **When things are good, go with it;** ride the crest. Keep in mind that there will also be times when things will not be so good, even though you may have done everything to make it right. Once again, your situation rests directly on your shoulders and it is your responsibility, even though there may be outside factors such as company buy-outs, Chapter 11 declarations, new management, or poor company financials. Smart investors make money when the stock market goes down. The best salespeople thrive under adversity. It can be done and is done regularly by the top 20 percent of any sales force. Just Do It!

• **When working as a sales executive,** as in all of life, remember that nothing is forever. Anticipate that everything will change. Always have a plan B.

• **Listen and be observant for warning signals** of problems and future problems within your company. Often you can avoid problems by knowing about them in advance and acting on that knowledge. You can never know too much. A fortune cookie I got recently said, "A danger foreseen is half avoided." A great quote in a great cookie!

• **Be your own sales manager** and never be dishonest with yourself. Know when things are good and when   they are bad. As I said at the start of this chapter, sales is not for everybody.

To be a successful salesperson, you need the Essence of Success: a positive attitude, a willingness to work hard, and the ability to instill confidence. And you need to avoid fear, excuses, and procrastination.

And you need those things now!

chapter two

Your Management, Your Company

"Whether you think you can, or you think you can't,
you're right."
— Henry Ford

Throughout this book, you will hear me stress mindset. To me, mindset includes your attitude and your effort — how you think about things and how hard you are willing to work to get them. A friend of mine says success isn't determined by "will power" it's determined by "want power." How badly you want to be successful, and how much effort you put into getting that success, is what determines what happens. If you don't really want something hard enough to do what you must to get it, you really don't want it. That decision is yours and yours alone. I can't make it for you. Your mother, your father, your spouse, your friend, or your neighbor can't make you successful. Nobody but you can want success strongly enough to get it. It's you and your mindset that determine your result.

But to be honest, almost always even your mindset isn't enough. Let me give you an example.

As much as we are talking about you being the sole sales professional, in the real world, sales is a team effort. That means even the best salesperson can fail if they are in the wrong environment; or if they are on a weak and ineffective team.

If you're a fan of pro sports, the NFL for example, you know that every year teams select the best college players to try out for their team. The NFL team with the worst record gets first pick. And how do they pick? The best player available or the one that fits their need. The draft was set up that way to help the worst teams get better. Sometimes it works spectacularly. But way too many times, even the best player can't be successful if the team he plays for — let me say it — stinks. The history of the draft is littered with the fallen bodies of "best players" who failed. Those players either found themselves in a poor environment that didn't help them grow and get better, or too much was expected of them too soon, or they weren't actually good enough to be a professional.

All that means even if your mindset to become a successful salesperson is good, if the company you work for doesn't support you and help you grow, you can easily fail — perhaps, through no fault of your own.

The difference between the Real World of Sales and getting drafted by the NFL, is that YOU get to choose the team you'd like to play for. You get to look at their record, their reputation, their training programs, and your potential teammates. And then you get to choose to seek a position with them or not. When you get an interview and you walk in the door, two things happen.

> **1. You are seeking information** about the quality of the company and determining if you think they are a fit to help you become successful.

> **2. They are evaluating you** to see if you can help them become more successful than they currently are.

I was very fortunate to begin my sales career and become a high-performing sales professional at Xerox Corporation. Many of the sales concepts that have carried me through my career were established during the time I worked for Xerox

Before working there, I had little sales experience. My plan had been to get a Masters Degree and then go to Law School. But while looking for a job to pay for those dreams, I applied at Xerox and they convinced me to accept a job in sales. But they didn't just hire me and put me in the starting lineup. Instead, they trained me thoroughly in their very competitive industry. That effort on their part altered my mindset and I found myself paying back their efforts by working as hard as I possibly could. As I was paying them back, I was solidifying the mindset that would carry me throughout the rest of my career.

In 1979, I was "Rookie of the Year" and ranked third overall in the Cleveland branch. For the next two years, I lead that same Cleveland branch in sales. My performance surprised even me! While the majority of my success was determined by my own efforts, I know for certain that the degree of success I achieved was directly related to the quality of the organization for which I worked. My advice to you based on what I learned is: Never underestimate the value of a quality sales organization.

To be selected to work for a quality company should be the goal of any qualified salesperson. If you have chosen the right company to work for, you won't be sorry. But how do you know about the inner workings of a company before you actually experience working there yourself? You talk to the people who do work there. Or who used to.

Ask them:

- How are sales members treated?
- Did they teach you enough about your products before you were put in the field?
- Did they teach you about their competition, their good points as well as their less-than-perfect aspects?
- Do they have a support staff and how would you rate it?
- Does support team satisfy all customer requests and requirements?
- Does the support staff support sales personnel fully?
- Would you rate the company as being ethical with employees as well as with customers?
- If you were looking for a sales job today, would you apply here knowing what you do now?

Not knowing the negatives before you wind up working for a company could result in a hasty job turnover that will show up on your resume. In a resume, quick job turnovers raise red flags, causing future potential employers to wonder if they should hire you or not.

In the perfect world, you want to work for the perfect company that sells the perfect product. You want to report to a perfect a manager who is motivating as well as understanding. This is the description of sales nirvana.

In the real world, having all those positive elements occur at the same time seldom happens. When you are fortunate enough to find yourself in sales heaven, don't even think of changing jobs. Ride out the crests and valleys and enjoy the ride. The only certainty in sales is change itself.

At one time, I was working for a very good company for a long time. During a working day, I received a phone call from a recently-hired Vice President of Sales of a well-known technology company. He made an offer to me on the phone to join his sales team. His offer would have upgraded my base salary by 50% and increased my commission by the same 50%.

I researched this company by looking at their website and speaking to one of their top-selling sales people. I decided to accept the offer.

Little did I know what I was getting into! Later, I discovered this company was having extensive financial problems, which was why they had added 50% more highly-experienced, successful salespeople; and why a new Senior Vice President of Sales had just been hired. Within six short months, the company declared Chapter 11 and announced a reduction in the work force of almost 60% of their existing employees.

No one saw this coming, but this situation interrupted several sales professionals' successful careers with unemployment.

Obviously, even the pre-hire homework I did wasn't perfect.

In hindsight, in addition to the tough questions listed above, I should also have asked:
- Why did the company just hire a new Senior Vice President of Sales?
- How have your sales been this year?
- Tell me about your recent sales personnel turnover.

I simply saw the increase in earnings and wanted to believe this was a great opportunity. It was not.

THE SALES MANAGER

The sales manager has a very important position in every organization. He or she is the traffic controller; the person who monitors, trains, motivates, hires, and ultimately fires all sales personnel. He or she can make or break a salesperson's current job, if not their entire career.

Because of the power a sales manager has, it is essential for them to be firm, fair, and consistent. If he or she is not, there is a risk that the sales department may not realize its true potential. The morale of a staff under such a sales manager may be low and lacking in enthusiasm — hardly qualities to inspire people or generate sales.

The success of any sales organization rests to a great extent on the ability of the sales manager to keep the troops focused and motivated.

Many notable sales organizations only hire sales managers from within their sales ranks. The upside of this is that strong sales performers are rewarded for their sales accomplishments. The knowledge of this potential reward is a carrot that drives success for many sales personnel. The stick side of the equation, however, is some of the best sales performers do not make great sales managers. Skill at selling does not always translate into skill at managing.

To be successful, Sales Managers should make these commitments to the sales team:
- Respect and Fair Treatment
- Total Support and Consultation
- Enthusiasm
- Structure and Direction
- Professional Growth and Career Development
- Sincerity and Willingness to Help
- Unwillingness to Tolerate Unjustifiable Non-Performance
- Commitment to Success

Sales Managers have the right to expect these commitments from their sales team members:
- Respect and Cooperation
- Positive Attitude
- Professionalism
- Support for Individual Members as Well as the Team
- High Activity Levels
- Fulfill All Job Requirements
- Ethical Behavior at All Times
- Dedication to Succeed

These commitments, undertaken by both the sales professional and the sales manager, are the social equivalent of "marriage" vows. It is important to honor these commitments at all times to keep the bond between sales personnel and the company strong. When this *marriage* ends — as it most certainly will at some time — the person hurt most is usually you. Don't be the cause of your own downfall. Honor your commitments!

Here is a situation I experienced. I became employed by another large company whose sales management, I soon discovered, intimidated their sales teams. This group of managers had no patience to develop their reps. Frequently, they would scream at them in an attempt to push sales, usually at the end of a sales quarter. During each quarter, the sales manager was nowhere to be seen by the sales reps. Once in a great while he would attend sales calls. His yelling was very demotivating, clearly contributing to their low sales numbers.

In another company, sales people were encouraged to uncover new sales opportunities in the territories of their fellow sales team members. There were always negative feelings shared by these sales reps toward their management and the company in general. As a result, the company's sales volumes were low and morale was equally low.

In any and every company, there is a direct connection between low sales volume, poor sales training, and badly managed companies. If you see one of these situations in a company you are considering working for, you can predict the other two are also likely present. Before you join any prospective company, you need to check on all these potential red flags. Do your homework well!

chapter three

Developing Your Action Plan, Territory, and Time Management

In the last chapter, I ended with a string of sad tales about working for bad sales managers. I know, it sounds like I had a lot of them but trust me, I left out most of the really bad stories and experiences. Like the alcoholic superman, the anger management guy, the prisoner interrogator, and the manager who suffered from bipolar disorder.

Sometimes, it seems like I went from one devil to another. And if I were to tell you everything about every bad sales manager and system, you'd wonder how I made it successfully through four decades in sales.

But I did. Through those experiences I figured out how to live, prosper, and advance my career. Learning how to overcome obstacles like that is what qualifies me to write this book.

The solution I came up with may sound simple but in the real world, it all boils down to one concept — planning. It is my sincere belief that no one, and that means you, should have to go out into their territory with no planning. I know because that's exactly how I started. I went out far too many times without a real plan. But when I began to create and follow a plan is when my successful sales life started to blossom.

So, if that sounds good to you, pay attention.

PLANNING

Success in Sales begins with a positive attitude, an excellent sales organization, and a sales manager who is supportive, motivating, and understanding. The support, direction, and training provided by the employing company means everything to a sales professional, especially to the beginner. The quality of the marriage between the sales organization and the salesperson will determine the result: either a successful future or the crashing conclusion of a career. To make sure your sales career gets off on the right foot, you must become proactive, and not merely a reactive responder.

Being proactive requires the creation of a personal business plan designed to create a meaningful quota. Just like companies have business plans, you must too, regardless of whether you are a solitary sales person, work for a small company, or are employed by a large Fortune 500 Corporation with a huge sales force.

Being successful requires that this plan be put into place immediately, not the second week on the job. You should place yourself on a challenging performance plan from the get-go, lest complacency sets in and company management places you on a plan of theirs. If that occurs, it's never good news for you. It usually means you only have a short time — normally between thirty and ninety days — to hit some hefty numbers or be given a pink slip.

The real outcome of most performance plans is that you will have that short amount of time to find a new job. If on day one in your sales job, you put yourself on your challenging plan, you will have the confidence of knowing that you will most likely succeed.

Success, however, should not be at all costs. Your plans and your actions need to remain ethical. For example, don't try to sell something you don't have or which you know you cannot deliver. Every customer is an elephant: they never forget! If you knowingly take advantage of a customer, they will remember; and most customers talk to other potential customers. I'm sure you have heard of the term grapevine.

The grapevine exists; and nowhere is it stronger than in the business community. If you do things right, your credibility will be known. But if you do things wrong, are not honest, and/or do not keep your commitments with customers, that also will be known.

In certain situations — due to some set of uncontrollable circumstances — one's job may not evolve as both the salesperson and the employer envision. Sometimes, even after every effort to do the right thing at the right time for the right reason, things just don't work out. If that should happen, walk away knowing you did the best that could be done. It is vital to leave an organization with the essence of who you are, with a reputation as a hard-working, focused, and honest professional. Maintaining your reputation, integrity and pride (RIPP) will ensure that you Rest In Peace by knowing that you did everything you could do to succeed.

Keep this in mind, too — it's never a good idea to take a sales job with the idea that you will leave it shortly. Always plan to remain employed by the same sales organization for a minimum of three to five years. An employment record made of durations of this length demonstrates a stable work history, which increases your value on the open job market. Turnover is never a good thing for the salesperson or the organization. For you, it means starting again to learn a new company and their culture, a new product, and a new territory. For the prospective employer it means the time and money they will invest in you — and good companies do invest in you — will not be wasted. It will show an ROI (return on investment) that will be to their benefit.

Most importantly, don't put yourself in the position of having to leave from a current sales position against your wishes. If you want control of your future, take charge of your choices today. Create a business plan for yourself from day one.

> ### WHEN THINGS GO WRONG, MAINTAIN YOUR RIPP
>
> Your Reputation, Integrity, and Professional Pride (RIPP) are important characteristics that tell those around you that you are worthy. They are the backbone of a successful career for the sales executive, the sales manager, and even the owner or board member. Your RIPP can never be taken from you. You don't lose it when you leave a position. The only way to lose your RIPP is through your weakness, inappropriate behavior, or sloppy and inattentive work practices.
>
> By maintaining your RIPP, you will continue to have access to one of the most important and valuable elements of long-term success in sales: your large, personal Contact List of happy and loyal customers who, as long as you sustain your RIPP, will continue to work with you even if you depart from your current employer.

CREATING YOUR
BUSINESS PLAN

When establishing goals, be realistic. With some effort, almost everyone can achieve their sales goals. The successful salesperson, however, sets goals that are just slightly beyond the reach of his/her everyday effort. By setting slightly higher goals, successful people push themselves and stretch their abilities to new levels of achievements. Eventually these higher goals become easier to achieve, and even higher goals are set. In this method, the salesperson pushes themselves up the sales ladder of success. This is the mindset required to be successful in sales.

But how does one set a goal? It's simple, work backwards. Working backwards means that you start with the end in mind— what do you want to achieve? Determine your sales in terms of revenue, profit margin and/or units sold. Since most sales professionals close about one-third of all their opportunities, you will need three times as many opportunities in your sales funnel to reach your target goal. This closure rate is not simply a function of the sales person's inability to close. In the real world of sales, all sorts of things happen that can prevent you from making the sale, including: tabling of corporate projects, lack of funding, changeover in management within the account, company audits, or even company politics in which a high level executive within your prospective company has a relationship with one of your competitors. The key to meeting and exceeding goals is to always have a sales funnel with three times the number of potential accounts required to achieve your desired goal.

To fill a sales funnel of this size requires work. Some prospects can be cultivated from your existing account base, if you have been assigned one. But to fill your sales funnel requires the hardest work of all: prospecting. In all sales scenarios, the critical portion of being successful with your business plan is the expenditure of time required to uncover new opportunities. The formula that made me successful at Xerox Corporation, for example, was to average at least one hundred new sales calls a week. That's twenty direct conversations over the telephone every day, and mostly with new accounts! This successful formula may be diagrammed in simple terms, as follows:

THE FORMULA FOR SUCCESS

The old paradigm for sales used to be:

- 100 cold calls to
- 10 face-to-face meetings to
- 1 sale.

By the way, when I say cold *calls* I am not limiting you to telephone *calls*. Today, people respond to a variety of media: phone calls, texts, email, LinkedIn® contacts, Facebook messenger, Tweets, Instagram, etc. Meeting people at conventions, conferences, meet and greets, and so forth are also acceptable cold calls. For simplicity in this book, I will always refer to these interactions as calls. But know that *calls* means all that I've mentioned and any and all that might arrive in our ever-changing digital world.

The new paradigm looks like this:

- 100 Cold Calls to
- 10 Suspects to
- 3 Qualified Prospects with Completed Proposals to
- 1 Sale.

The new paradigm qualifies the suspects (those capable of needing your product or service) into qualified prospects for which you complete a sales proposal. This distinction does two things.
1. It allows you to maintain a sub-list of folks to revisit at a later time.
2. It reinforces the necessity for you to generate completed proposals.

Keep in mind that these are weekly goals. Every week. All year long.

In addition to goals, your business plan should detail the source of your leads (business partners, customer referrals, etc.). Once you have put your plan into writing in great detail, show it to your direct sales manager and ask him or her if your proposed plan is acceptable, realistic, and can be achieved. Ask for mentoring in revising and reworking your plan's components. In this way, your sales manager should be more committed to your success under his or her direction.

Once your goals are established and approved, you need to develop your action plans: what exactly will you do and when will you do it to achieve the elements of your goal?

By creating a Business Plan, getting input and suggestions from your sales manager, and creating the specific action steps, you will go a long way towards not only achieving your goals but exceeding them. At the same time, you will almost certainly avoid being placed on a performance improvement plan (PIP) by your management.

THE PLAN TO SUCCEED AND THE PLAN TO FAIL

Business Plan > Action Plan < Performance Plan

The functional heart of successful planning —the document that tells you what to do and when to do it — is the Action Plan. Action Plans are either created as the logical result of your business plan, or they are created for you as part of the Performance Plan on which your company has put you. No matter how you arrive there, you will have an action plan. Arriving at an Action Plan of your own volition is always the better choice. To do that means you have to start by developing your Business Plan.

BUSINESS PLAN

Many companies, regardless of size, request that their employees create their own individual business plan to be reviewed by their direct managers. This appears to be a sensible approach since the development of your sales territory should be viewed as the development of your own business. In other words, a successful salesperson looks at their territory as the boundaries of their own company. They will consider it their job to make their company the dominant organization in that region. I have always felt that the salesperson doing the actual selling is best suited to create such a plan, subject to approval by management. If it's your territory, it ought to be your plan to conquer it.

Business plans should include highlighting product and competitive education, learning the company's culture, and doing what is necessary to exceed sales quotas.

As in most things, planning is a requirement for success. Take a few days in advance of making your first calls to set up your Business Plan.

Be familiar with your company information, your website, and social media links if necessary, and be prepared to pass that information to the prospect. Disorganization can and will cost you hours of lost time, confusion, and high-blood pressure. Set yourself up to win!

Following is a template I created to set up my most current business plan. Feel free to use it word-for-word, or to modify it as you see fit.

—————————— · —————————— ·

(Year) Proposed Territory Plan
Presented By:
(Your Name) (Assigned Territory)
. . . .

OVERVIEW
The following is my proposed business plan designed to surpass my sales quota as (Major Account Manager) at (your company). I will base this projection upon the development of many current and non-existing customer accounts. In light of this, I will display high activity levels involving the penetration of new accounts. To begin, I almost always follow the successful formula that has allowed me to over-achieve my quota during my extensive sales career. If followed properly, this program will work. The main ingredients that make this formula work are as follows:
• Hard work (a given)
• Product knowledge
• Knowledge of the competition
• The ability to rapidly qualify 30-50 accounts and to develop a legitimate sales funnel

After this initial assessment of those accounts, have a backup plan to contact another 30-50 suspect accounts to qualify as well
I will always stay focused, stay positive, and be relentless in pursuing my sales objectives

The following is my formula:
• Average 15 - 20 direct contacts, new and existing, per day.
• 1-2 face- to-face meetings (in-person or remote) per day, at least 8 per week.
• Monday can be an organizational/office day, to effectively set up my week. This will be comprised of setting my appointments

for the coming week along with following up on all necessary customer, office, and other sales-related objectives.

The remainder of the week, I will plan to be in the territory conducting face-to-face meetings. I will work closely with our (manufacturers / partners) like (company) and (company).

Most importantly, I will continually pursue large sales opportunities to exceed my business objectives. I plan to offer those partner organizations great value, utilizing my large Contact List of high-level customer contacts in the territory.

Further, I will provide the greatest service and follow-up to both my potential clients as well as my business partners. By this process, I will create a value proposition that cannot be duplicated by my competition.

. . . .

1. GOALS & OBJECTIVES
This section will display my goals and objectives broken out into different time elements. My goals will be based on the following categories:
- Financial
- Business & Professional Accomplishments
- Personal & Professional Development
- Other

3 MONTHS
- Financial: Obtain 100% of my first quarter revenue and profit margin objectives
- Financial: Compile all account information and evaluate projected revenue streams.
- Business & Professional Accomplishments: Manage activities, face-to-face meetings, proposals generated, and replenish the pipeline when necessary. Learn and develop value-added business relationships with all appropriate manufacturers, resellers, and partners, if applicable.
- Personal & Professional Accomplishments: Develop a continuous technical and professional training schedule for the current year involving all company product and service offerings.
- Personal & Professional Accomplishments: Fully understand the business model and culture of (your company) Management.
- Other: Always strive to understand the requirements of the upper management and teammates I work with and for.

- Other: Remain open by learning new productive ways to approach my responsibilities.
- Other: Always be a team player with no private agenda.

6 MONTHS
- Constantly review where quota revenue volumes are coming from for the year.
- Continue to penetrate targeted accounts to uncover new potential.
- Fully understand the (your company) product offerings and continue all training courses designated.
- Strive to secure at least three to five new active accounts with revenue potential.
- Continue to understand your company culture and business practices. Ask questions when you have uncertainty.
- Keep income-planning in the forefront. Look to be at a minimum obtainment of 100% of sales quota, year-to-date.
- Fully understand Management's criteria of all expectations involving my performance.

9 MONTHS
- Strive to reach my sales quota and/or develop new accounts to reach or exceed it.
- Continue all training that was established in the first six months.
- Evaluate my road map of the last nine months with respect to exceeding my quota.
- On track to reach or exceed 75% of my sales quota.

12 MONTHS
- Have exceeded my sales quota at excellent margins.
- Set up account penetration to exceed quota in (the next year).
- Earn President's Club Status, if applicable.

24 MONTHS
- Exceed quota once again, but at an even greater level.
- Set up an even better year (the next year).
- Fully understand all new elements of your industry.

60 MONTHS
- Exceed sales-quota.
- Earn fifth straight trip to President's Club, if applicable.
- Use my experience and knowledge to consistently assist other sales reps to reach their goals.

- Continue to evolve my skills both in the market and with the technology.
- Bring in new quality accounts worthy of national recognition.
- Support Management and their sales promotions.

. . . .

2. PERSONAL VALUE STATEMENT

My value proposition is to provide the best possible solution that delivers the greatest technical, business and financial results for my customers. If I do not have a proper solution for their requirements, I will tell them so.

I am dedicated to self-improvement. I will further my overall knowledge for the greater understanding of (my specific industry) involving solutions-based areas (pertinent to my industry) along with product knowledge and technologies coordinated with or integrated into (your company). I will embrace all management direction, both professional and technical, to the best of my ability.

3. ACCOUNT OPPORTUNITIES

The following 70 suspect accounts will provide the backup for my initial 30-50 focused working accounts. This plan covers (assigned territory and/or account listings). I will make territorial adjustments according to geographical / account assignments.

These accounts are listed as follows:

SUSPECT ACCOUNT LIST for (current year)
    (list accounts here)

TARGETED HIT LIST OF ACCOUNTS (BY CITY OR OTHER UNIT)
(List each City)
(List accounts under each city)

. . . .

CONCLUSION

This is a 20,000-foot preliminary overview of my annual Business Plan as an Account Executive for (your company). I fully believe that this initial plan will serve as the necessary road map to successfully build my assigned territory into the profitable business unit envisioned by (your company) management. During the course of (year), this plan shall be continuously extended, lengthened, and more accurately compiled with the assistance and interaction of (your company) management.

Thank you in advance for your consideration and I look forward to our next steps.
Regards, (your name)

· ————————— · ————————— ·

ACTION PLAN OVERVIEW

An action plan is a set of specific activities required to carry out the generalized business plan.
Your action plan should include these four elements:
1. Action Plan Review Session with Direct Sales Manager
2. Territory Account Overview
3. Strategies to implement your activities
4. Goals & Objectives to meet or exceed the number of orders and projected revenue

These Action Plan Elements should be fairly understandable to both seasoned and beginning salespeople in any industry. While every company may have different names for these elements, their functions will exist to some degree in every situation. Understanding these elements using Selling in the Real World terminology will help you understand and function perfectly in any corporate system.

Let's take a closer look at the second element, Territory Account Overview.

TERRITORIES

Every salesperson will have a territory in which to work. The territory can be geographical, industry-based, or unlimited. Prospects and customers for each sales person are part of their territory. Some accounts will be inherited, some will be generated by the sales person, some will come from leads supported by inside sales professionals (or support-team members), and some will come from online lead generating funnels.

Inside sales folks rarely make outside face-to-face sales calls. The leads generated by the inside sales staff are usually turned over to the outside sales people.

Outside sales professionals fall into two classifications: Geographical Representative and Major Account Manager.

The Geographical Representative has a sales territory defined by boundaries located within a geographic area. These territories are often set up by zip codes or some geographic subdivisions. The Geographical Representative may have some existing account or may have to develop that territory from scratch. That is, within the salesperson's territory, there may not be any existing business or clients.

The Major Account Manager (MAM) handles large accounts normally headquartered in a large city or region. Rather than being defined by location, these accounts are defined by sales volume or monetary potential. Often these are Fortune 500 companies. These companies may have multiple locations but most buying decisions originate at the main corporate office. The Major Account Manager usually has a longer sales cycle and must employ a highly structured, strategic sales plan to attack the multi-layers of corporate politics.

The MAM usually has existing accounts and does not have to build a territory from scratch. However, he or she is still expected to secure new accounts and expand the revenues within existing accounts. In most companies, Geographical Reps can graduate to Major Account sales, since there is greater detail and attention required when selling Fortune 500 accounts. As such, to become a MAM can be viewed as a promotion from the position of Geographical Representative.

When a salesperson inherits an outside sales territory, it is advisable to begin by:

1. Determining if there are any hot accounts or opportunities that were not closed by the previous salesperson.

2. Following up on those previous hot accounts and opportunities. It is always more advantageous to close immediate business than to spend time prospecting for new.

3. Closing the sale of any and all outstanding hot accounts and opportunities before the competition steps in and takes away the business.

Understanding the successes and failures of your predecessor is an often overlooked practice. The information gathered and analyzed can provide two insights.

1. The things that worked that you should do more of.

2. The things that didn't work that you should fix or ignore.

If you are assigned existing customers, contact them immediately, and plan to visit them as soon as possible. An existing account can explain the strengths and weaknesses of your company. Your competition already has knowledge of your company's shortcomings and by gathering this information you will develop the correct responses to future customers

FOUR TIME MANAGEMENT TIPS

1. **Always plan sales calls** in the same geographical vicinity during each half or full day. Unnecessary driving is poor time management. Time is your only non-renewable resource. Never waste it.

2. **Be able to explain** your action plan to anyone who asks. Back up your plan with facts and a personal commitment to execute it to the best of your ability.

3. **Never allow anyone** to question your commitment to personal organization.

4. **Always plan** for your own success. Success is a result of executing a well-thought-out action plan with management buy-in. Failure is assuming everything is all right. Without documented assurances that it is, more times than not, it isn't.

ACTIVITY LEVELS

- Appointments, cold calls per day average, presentations, and proposals per month
- New Sales and Marketing Ideas or Techniques
- Update skills, knowledge, and improve your singular core
- Create and maintain online links that support you, your products, and your services

FINAL THOUGHTS

1. **You are your own best sales manager.** Keep yourself on track, maintain a positive attitude, and stay highly motivated. Listen to what's being said and take it as constructive criticism. Use everything you can to improve your performance and results.

2. **To be successful,** action plans should be created in cooperation with your direct supervisor and receive his or her approval and buy-in before they are put in place. Having an action plan in place during the first 90 days is essential and critical. Following it and achieving your goals is necessary for your success.

chapter four

Laying out the Requirements

SALES AUTOMATION TOOLS

Sales Automation Tools did not come into existence by either spontaneous creation, or as the brain child of one person's thinking. Sales Automation Tools are the digital, online offspring of forms and documents created by hand, typewriter, and word processors and used successfully for generations of sales people of all types, skills, and abilities. Understanding where these tools came from can help you exploit them from a strategic perspective. Almost anyone can learn the tactics of a Sales Automation Tool and make it function. But when you understand the strategies from which these tools were born, you can push them to their ultimate ability — and isn't that how you want everything to work for you when you're Selling in the Real World?

As of the date of this book, the Sales Automation Tool of choice seems to be Sales Force. Once we learn where that came from, we'll take a look at how it can make your life better, easier, and more productive.

Let's go back in time and look at the forms I developed years ago. And once you understand the strategies I used to create them, you can successfully transfer that knowledge to make the Sales Automation Tool of your choice produce the results you laid out in your business plan and action plan.

SALES PAPERWORK.
NECESSARY EVIL OR NECESSARY GOOD?

Well, the answer to that question is: yes.

I recall a sales position I once held at a major corporation. Every Monday morning at 8:30 A.M., our sales team conducted a weekly conference call. In the afternoon we had one-on-one meetings with our sales manager. Each Friday, all the sales reps were required to complete four separate sets of activity and prospect reports. Monday through Friday we had a corporate on-line prospect forecasting report due by the close of the day! At the end of every month, we were required to complete a monthly report detailing all our activities of the previous thirty days and forecast our anticipated activities for the next month. Because of the paperwork requirements, we had only three days available to schedule face-to-face meetings with potential customers! Needless to say, paperwork requirements like that are not in the best interest of sales people with assigned quotas. To make matters worse, management expected paperwork to be completed after normal working hours. This resulted in a sixty-hour workweek and caused low morale, reduced sales, and, eventually, sales burnout by the sales team. As you would expect, the over-riding concern in each salesperson's mind was on completing their paperwork instead of on creating sales and/or developing potential customers.

So that you don't find yourself in a situation dominated by overwhelming paperwork always ask about required paperwork before accepting a new sales position. Try to analyze the company's paperwork requirements to determine if it's designed for you, the sales professional, to be more organized and strategic within your accounts, or if it's a mechanism for the sales manager to cover his/her own backside. You should know that when a system is designed to protect a manager, it's often YOU that suffers in the end.

GOOD PAPERWORK

Good paperwork helps to create a track to run on and enables you to monitor your success and short-comings in your territory. The forms on the following pages may be utilized by both the beginner as well as the polished sales professional trying to get back on track. Sometimes, when a salesperson becomes successful, filling out the paperwork may seem tedious and unnecessary. Many of my sales managers told me at various times in my career, that when I was ahead of plan, that they didn't care if I filled it out or even where I was or what I was doing during the working day.

I never took them up on their offer. Partly because I knew I would be cheating myself, and partly because I saw first-hand what happened to those who no longer followed these protocols and procedures. It was not uncommon to see a successful sales rep milking a large, revenue producing account and doing nothing else. You can almost guess the sequence of events. The golden-goose-account dries up, goes south, or the economy gets soft. Suddenly the rep is fighting to find new accounts as well as to keep his job!

If hard work and following protocol made me successful, why would I change my behavior once I became successful? I wouldn't. And I always encourage sales professionals to stay on track, to continue to do all the right things, and to use as many of these tracking methodologies as work for you. I also suggest not using any procedure or paperwork that simply turns into busy work. If something doesn't work or no longer works, don't use it. Requiring paperwork from a sales staff simply to cover the sales manager's backside is not productive for the sales manager, the sales professional, or the organization for which they work. Use these forms to help guide your sales process and make you successful. Only utilize the forms that will, in fact, assist you.
Most of these charts and forms are now automated and used in Sales Force Automation (SFA) applications and Customer Relations Management (CRM) tools. Whether you access them electronically via software or the web, or manually with pen and paper, understanding and using these charts and forms are essential core elements in any sales environment. This is covered in detail in the next chapter.

TRACKING FORMS

Tracking forms are designed to help you monitor your activity levels and keep you on track as you complete the elements of your action plan. On the following pages are some you might find useful.

THE WEEKLY ACTIVITY FORM

By keeping a detailed list of your weekly activities on this form, you will discover what you are doing right or what you may be doing wrong. For example, if your appointment or call activity is high but you are not closing enough business, then analyzing what you've put on the form may indicate you might not be contacting the right person, might not be qualifying properly, or might not be providing accurate, hard-hitting proposals. Or, if applicable, your product demonstrations may need work.

Weekly Activity Report

SALESMAN			TERRITORY		WEEK ENDING	ACCOMPLISHMENTS									
DAY	TIME	CALL or ACTIVITY	EMAIL or PHONE	CONTACT NAME TITLE	RESULT	NEW CALL	CALL BACK	USER VISIT	DEMO	PROPOSAL ISSUED	SIGNED ORDER ($$ VOLUME)	SURVEY (HRS)	INSTALLATION (HRS)	OFFICE (HRS)	NON-WORK (HRS)

MASTER PROSPECT LIST

This form is your sales funnel or pipeline. Keeping it current and accurate is crucial for your success in your territory. You should have at least thirty active to fifty targeted accounts that you have identified, researched, and/or contacted.

Master Prospect List

ACCOUNT NAME	ADDRESS	PHONE/ EMAIL	DOLLAR AMOUNT	PROPOSED EQUIPMENT	DECISION MAKER	TARGET CLOSE

ACCOUNT PROFILE CALL REPORT

This report contains the detailed breakdown of each of your top prospects. Keeping this information updated after discussing these accounts with your sales manager and others on your sales team will help you better understand where you are in the sales cycle for each account and what to do to make them closable, profitable accounts.

GOOD MANAGERS PROVIDE ON-SITE OVERSIGHT

Good sales managers usually plan to spend two days a month traveling with their direct-reporting sales reps to observe the habits, practices, and tendencies of each rep and to meet in person some of the rep's top prospects. This could also be accomplished through an online video session.

Account Profile – Call Report

Account Name: _____ Salesperson:_____

Address: _____

Date of Contract: _____

Source of Lead: _____

Phone: _____

Email: _____

Present System/Product: _____

_____

Purchase: [] Lease [] Rental [] Expires: _____

Proposed System/Product: _____

_____

Purchase: [] Lease [] Rental [] Expires: _____

Basic Configurations: _____

Options: _____

Competition: 1. _____ 2. _____ 3. _____

Names of Department Decision-makers

_____ _____

_____ _____

_____ _____

_____ _____

Contact Dates: 1. _____ 2. _____ 3. _____

                      4. _____ 5. _____ 6. _____

Demonstration Dates: 1. _____ 2. _____

Proposal Dates: 1. _____ 2. _____

Estimated Sales Cycle: 0-30 ___ 31-60 ___ 61-90 ___

Strengths   1. _____

            2. _____

            3. _____

            4. _____

Weakness   1. _____

            2. _____

            3. _____

            4. _____

WEEKLY PRIORITIES FORM

This is an organizational tool that allows you to view your schedule for the upcoming week. This form can also list topics of conversation to discuss with your management or support staff.

Weekly Priorities

Name: _____

Week of: _____

Activities:

1. _____
2. _____
3. _____
4. _____
5. _____
6. _____
7. _____
8. _____
9. _____

Request for Assistance:

1. _____
2. _____
3. _____
4. _____

Travel Schedule

TIME	MON	TUE	WED	THU	FRI
8 am					
NOON					

DAILY TO-DO LIST

Most successful people have a To-Do List on which they prioritize the things they intend to accomplish that day. A To-Do List is not a plan, it is not a goal, it is not objectives. It is simply a list that has been prioritized so that the owner of the list can spend his or her time accomplishing the most important things first, thus generating the greatest return on their investment of time and effort.

Your To-Do List may be a separate piece of paper or a page in your planner or electronic platform.

Things to Do Today

Date : _____

Day: _____

THINGS TO DO	RESULTS	COMMENTS

"A" Priority:

1. _____   _____
2. _____   _____
3. _____   _____
4. _____   _____
5. _____   _____
6. _____   _____
7. _____   _____
8. _____   _____
9. _____   _____

"B" Priority:

1. _____   _____
2. _____   _____
3. _____   _____
4. _____   _____
5. _____   _____
6. _____   _____
7. _____   _____
8. _____   _____
9. _____   _____

People to Call or See:

1. _____   _____
2. _____   _____
3. _____   _____
4. _____   _____
5. _____   _____

UNDERSTANDING SALES FORCE AUTOMATION

Sales Force is an information and customer relationship management system that automates sales and sales management functions. It organizes customers, colleagues, suppliers, and so forth throughout the lifecycle of your relationship. In other words, it replaces the hard copies of all the forms and planners and records that were typically used by sales personnel with enhanced digital, online versions.

Because of this move to an online service, information can be observed by sales personnel, sales management, and company executives at any time of day from any location. This immediacy can have the effect of keeping sales personnel on track and focused on the day and days ahead so they can better move forward in the creation of new accounts and the management of existing accounts to help the sales professional achieve and exceed their goals.

As do many companies, Sales Force produces a variety of software programs like, Sales Cloud, Service Cloud, Data Cloud, Marketing Cloud, Chatter, Analytic Cloud, and Custom Cloud. While each of these has differences, they all follow the same line of productivity, integration, and automation and work in much the same way. Transferring your skill set from one to another is relatively simple.

Some of the functions that Sales Force has automated may include:

- Opportunities
- Forecasted revenues
- Closing dates
- Percentage of close ratio
- Sales activities
- Contact names
- Deliverables and proposal generation
- Product and service compilations
- Managed sales process
- Quota obtainments
- Territory management
- Performance support
- Social Media integration
- Third party vendors
- Customer data sources

While Sales Force is the most popular sales automation tool in use today, it may not have all the forms, lists, and tools you will need to be successful. One such application is the meeting invitation or appointment scheduler. Microsoft Outlook and Exchange are two of the better-known cloud-based applications that can provide this service.

SCHEDULING APPOINTMENTS

The most successful people have and use a planning system, whether it's a program on their phone or a planner in their hand. The goal is to have with you a single record of all your past and future events. You should be able to insert notes pertinent to the specific clients, activities, and events of the day. The ability to look back at your notes at a later date is as valuable as the ability to look forward to your future schedule.

Depending on the culture of your company, you may be hooked into one company-wide, computer-controlled scheduling system that contains all appointments and out puts individual daily invitations and to-do lists.

Whatever system you choose, learn it, follow it, and use it as an important tool to stay on track.

OTHER REQUIREMENTS

Mondays are usually the best and most practical day for individual and team sales meetings. It is also a great day to attempt to set new appointments, complete necessary company documentation — hopefully that means sales orders — and to conduct team building, like training or brainstorming sessions.

For the most part, Tuesday through Friday of a normal business workweek should be set aside for scheduling face-to-face or virtual meetings with potential or existing customers. Never let paperwork or unscheduled office time take the place of being in front of customers. High sales activity usually equates to large revenue streams.

Keep in mind that email, texting, and cloud-based messaging systems can provide strong market penetration in your territory. These techniques are effective methods for uncovering new business and corresponding with both new and existing prospects.

REVIEW OF SALES ACTIONS and TO-DO LISTS

This is an outline of what a typical sales week might look like.

MONDAY OFFICE ACTIVITIES
- Morning Sales Team meeting
- Discuss new company policies, incentives, or training
- Review forecast for week
- Schedule new appointments and update paperwork
- Follow-up all sources of lead generation
- Set other days for face-to-face meetings during regular business hours

ONE-ON-ONE SESSIONS
- Update orders written
- Discuss plans for week
- Review activities of previous week

OTHER ACTIVITIES
- New or existing account email, texting, and messaging
- Create email, social media, texting campaigns
    1 Sales Team travel days
    2 Share ideas/techniques
    3 Learn/improve skills
- Team building as needed or requested
- Discuss and analyze the competition
- Professional selling and territory management training
- Brainstorming
- Discuss success cases
- Discuss new ideas, suggestions
- Discuss concerns

The right volume of well thought-out paperwork, sensibly administered, is a definite bonus. Too much paperwork, poorly designed, and badly administered, can be an inefficient nightmare.

NOTE TO SALES MANAGERS

Sales managers have a lot of responsibility. Not only must they fully understand the entire sales cycle, they must understand how to maneuver subordinates through it successfully. Sales managers must learn to recruit, hire, and train good talent. They must accept sales reps as individuals with unique responses to motivational techniques, yet learn to motivate each of them to overcome the pressures of the profession.

Successful Sales Managers must be something of a psychologist to generate positive results while keeping staff turnover to a minimum. For the entire sales team to be successful, sales managers must continually direct the sales team in the difficult and grueling task of prospecting.

Many sales personnel look at becoming a Sales Manager as the next step in their career. However, not all good salespeople make good managers. The characteristics of a sales manager require a greater degree of personal skills than simply exceeding sales quota.

If you are interested in Becoming a Great Sales Manager in the Real World,® you can contact me at sellingintherealworld.com/manager

chapter five

Social Selling

Social Selling is the term in Selling in the Real World that covers the methods of interpersonal communication we use in daily interactions with people. Those tools include both Social Media and Messaging Media.

Social Media includes Facebook, Instagram, LinkedIn®, Twitter, and other similar Internet-based communication tools.

Messaging Media includes Texting, Instant Messaging, YouTube, Blogging, and other similar Internet-based communication tools.

Because of the rapid changes in our technology-based world, new tools come into the market on a regular and constant basis. And no doubt by the time you read this, something else may have jumped up on the common-usage ladder. Likely that tool will fall into one of these two categories.

SOCIAL MEDIA

Wikipedia describes social media in this way:
> " ... *a group of Internet-based applications ... that allow for the creation of user-generated content . . . social media depend on mobile and web-based technologies to create highly interactive platforms through which individuals and communities, share, co-create, discuss, and modify user-generated content.*"

Some companies maintain business sites on Facebook and Twitter that are used mainly to drive consumer sales through awareness and discounts. Some do, however, have private pages intended to communicate with employees and/or customers. Each site will have its own rules and protocols determined by the company. Your interaction on such sites will be determined by and limited to company protocols.

When I first began my career in sales, we had three ways to communicate with clients — by letter, on the phone, and in person. I know, for some of you, that's a world you can't imagine. But to be successful at anything we do, we all have to learn and live with the world we have. And so I did.

Today, we all use a cell phone, email, texting, social media, and virtual meetings. And while the technology is different, what hasn't changed are the people involved. We still have sellers, and buyers, and manufacturers, and customers. And what also hasn't changed are the skills and talents of dealing with people, understanding their needs and wants, and providing them the solutions they need, want, and are willing to buy.
No matter what changes down the road — and based on my life experiences things will change even faster in the future than they have in the past — the essential ingredient of selling in the real world won't — how we interact with people.

FACEBOOK

Wikipedia says this about Facebook:
> *"Facebook is an American online social media and social networking service. After registering, users can create a profile revealing information about themselves. They can post text, photos and multimedia which are shared with any other users who have agreed to be their "friend", or, with a different privacy setting, with any reader. Users can also use various embedded apps, join common-interest groups, buy and sell items or services on Marketplace, and receive notifications of their Facebook friends' activities and activities of Facebook pages they follow."*

There are three kinds of Facebook accounts: Profile, Page, Group.

1.Profile is for individual users and is the most common. It is the prototype of what people visualize when they think of Facebook: photographs, groups of people addressing the camera, gags, jokes, and memes.

2. Page is for businesses and fan groups. Businesses have sites that promote directly to end users.

3. Groups are by made up of approved members with a common interest or goal. Often it is career-related but can be for animal rescue, artists, religious groups, or anyone who wishes to be connected only to people in certain categories of life. This can be a place for the sales professional to seek out those like him and or those who are interested in the product or service the salesperson is representing. Within the rules of Facebook, direct selling and promotions are permitted. Some pages offer products directly for sale to end users.

While Facebook contains many examples of people and users who do not connect with sales, there are many sites, pages, and groups that do. The thorough professional will take the time to find them, join those that have value to him or her, and use them to their advantage.

INSTAGRAM

Wikipedia says this about Instagram:
"Instagram is a free, online photo-sharing application and social network platform that ...allows users to edit and upload photos and short videos through a mobile app. Users can add a caption to each of their posts and use hashtags and location-based geotags to index these posts and make them searchable by other users within the app.... users can like, comment on and bookmark others' posts, as well as send private messages to their friends."

Instagram is also highly used by companies who want to promote their brand, products, and corporate involvement. Instagram says more than a million advertisers use Instagram to tell their story and create business. Instagram promotes the fact that 60% of people who interact with corporate Instagram posts discover products and services they were not previously aware of.

Being on Instagram is an opportunity for the Sales Professional to connect visually with potential clients and share success stories and testimonials from clients. Some products and services will work better on Instagram than others.

LINKEDIN®

The one site that has made important inroads into sales is LinkedIn®. As of 2021, LinkedIn® is the largest professional network with more than 740 million members in more than 200 countries.

The basic service is free but serious users take advantage of the pro version with its more targeted and adaptable options. Members connect with peers and potential clients, not to sell to them directly, but to create an environment of sharing information, opportunities, and solutions to problems with the long-term intention of creating buyers and sellers.

Users of LinkedIn®:
1. **Establish** their professional profile
2. **Connect** with people to create their own network based on their intentions
3. **Research** companies and their employees away from corporate-controlled website descriptions
4. **Find and connect** with new career opportunities
5. **Gently prospect** for sales opportunities
6. **Create lists** of personal and peer contacts, referred to as friends in other social media

Successful users of LinkedIn® do not use their contact lists for hard and direct sales. They intentionally search out high-level, qualified buyers with whom they can create a level of rapport that hopefully over time will lead to more direct opportunity for sales. I have heard some say that LinkedIn® is a "garden to be tended, not an orchard with low hanging fruit."

An important advantage of being on LinkedIn® is that potential customers/buyers can research you — your history, skills, and successes — before they interact with you on a one-on-one basis through LinkedIn® or in person. Members are best served to create meaningful, clear, and well-thought-out profiles with professional photos, text, and graphics. What you look like on LinkedIn® will determine what people think about you before they ever meet you. This is not a place for the unstructured references of Facebook.

An interesting feature of LinkedIn® is something called tagging. In this process, you create names for tags that define things you typically want to know about your client base and potential clients or customers. Each one of your contacts will have a series of custom fields that you determine and fill out that will allow you later to create the ability to search through all your customers to find, say, owners of businesses with fewer than ten employees. Or people who were introduced to you at meetings or parties. Or people who live in New Orleans. Or people who might like a referral for what you are selling.

The ability to search through tags of YOUR client base allows you to manipulate your information to get what you want out the information you have collected over time.

The tagging search could result in direct contacts from you to the people on the final list via email, text, or phone. A sample email or LinkedIn® Mail could go like this:

> *"Mr. O'Conner. I just uncovered this recently-released article from Microsoft explaining integrated software for CRM. I think you may find it helpful as you implement your five-year plan, which you and I discussed a few weeks ago. Please let me know your impression."*

As a result, your contact will likely feel obligated to respond. Once he does, you could answer:

> *"Thanks for your feedback on the Microsoft article about CRM. Glad it helped. Do you have about 30 minutes next week to discuss this information? Depending on your time, we could do this in person, on the phone, or online."*

Once you have met, remember to send a thank you note through LinkedIn®. It could be as simple as:

> *"It was great meeting you today. I look forward to hearing back from you regarding the key points we discussed"*

A FEW MORE LINKEDIN® CONSIDERATIONS

1. When you search a company, try to make contacts both vertically and horizontally as well as your target demos. You never know when knowing someone to the left, right, or above a future contact will be the key to getting through to your intended target.

2. You should try to join several groups that each have value to what you do and to whom you want to connect.

3. You should post new information, releases, and topics on a regular but non-annoying basis. Information must be valuable, relevant, valid, new, and not sales-oriented in nature. You are providing your insight and expertise, not pitching a sale!

4. LinkedIn® is used not only to find buyers, but also to find subject-matter experts, new employees, and partners in new and existing businesses.

5. Companies use LinkedIn® as a marketing tool to promote their business. You should be doing the same for you. What you say and do, and what your LinkedIn® page looks like, have a huge impact on your ability to Sell in the Real World.

TWITTER

Wikipedia says this about Twitter:

"Twitter is an American microblogging and social networking service on which users post and interact with messages known as "tweets." Registered users can post, like, and retweet tweets, but unregistered users can only read them. Users access Twitter through its website interface or its mobile-device application...Twitter is a some-to-many microblogging service, given that the vast majority of tweets are written by a small minority of users. Tweets are limited to 280 characters, audio and video tweets to 140 seconds."

Sales people use Twitter to make announcements to followers and to topics connected by hashtags. Announcements can be about new products and services, events, or happenings of a personal nature designed to create bonds of familiarity between the tweeter (salesperson) and the recipient (clients and/or potential clients). Direct sales are not the goal of using Twitter but of crafting relationships and driving followers to websites and/or events where sales are the goal.

MESSAGING MEDIA

TEXTING
Wikipedia says this about Texting

> *"Text messaging, or texting, is the act of composing and sending electronic messages, typically consisting of alphabetic and numeric characters, between two or more users of mobile devices, desktops/ laptops, or other type of compatible computer. Text messages may be sent over a cellular network, or may also be sent via an Internet connection.*
>
> *"Like e-mail and voicemail and unlike calls (in which the caller hopes to speak directly with the recipient), texting does not require the caller and recipient to both be free at the same moment; this permits communication even between busy individuals."*

Effective texting requires both the sender and the recipient to know and acknowledge each other's cell phone numbers. When used like this, texts can be about new sales information, dates of products or services release, discounts, offers, events, or simply sales follow up. Texting is an ideal way to keep customers informed of opportunities that could be to their advantage and to create and support the relationship between them and the sales professional.

When the sender of a text accesses a cell phone without the recipient's permission, knowledge, or approval, it is considered spam or a robo text (automated broadcast to random numbers generated by a computer program.) Such usage often results in the blocking of the number by the recipient which would prevent the sales person from making contact in the future even by the phone.

In recent years, the usage of texting (down from 1.3 Trillion per year in the US) has been diminished by Instant Messaging connected to social media like Facebook Messenger, LinkedIn® Messaging, WeChat, and WhatsApp. Instant Messaging requires both parties to belong to or have accounts with the same social media or use the same cell phone app. The main difference between IM and Texting is that IM happens in real time.

Word-wide, more people use their cell phones for texting than talking.

INSTANT MESSAGING

Wikipedia says this about Instant Messaging:

"Instant messaging (IM) technology is a type of online chat that offers real-time text transmission over the Internet…Instant Messaging…often uses a contact list…Some IM applications use push technology to provide real-time text, which transmits messages character by character as they are composed…advanced instant messaging can add file transfer, clickable hyperlinks, Voice over IP, or video chat much like the options in texting use a cell phone."

There is little effective difference between texting and Instant Messaging, the choice of which to use is up to the people involved. The concept of this one-to-one, real-time communication allows for immediate and personal interaction between sales professionals, customers (current or potential), or among peers.

Sending sales information via texting or IM to people is known as Direct Message Marketing.

One recent usage for sales professionals of texting and IM is to create

FAULTY FORECASTS: PINK SLIPS IN WAITING

False assumptions and poorly qualifying prospects equate to faulty forecasts. Faulty forecasts can quickly terminate your employment or eliminate you as a sales professional.

instant, private, and simultaneous communication between two people who find themselves on a live video interaction. In this manner they can have a conversation without bothering others or interfering with the video call.

EMAIL

There two levels of email usage involved in Selling in the Real World: Email marketing and email interaction.

EMAIL MARKETING

Wikipedia defines email marketing as:

"Email marketing is the act of sending a commercial message, typically to a group of people, using email. In its broadest sense, every email sent to a potential or current customer could be considered email marketing. It involves using email to send advertisements, request business, or solicit sales or donations. Email marketing strategies commonly seek to achieve one or more of three primary objectives, to build loyalty, trust, or brand awareness. The term usually refers to sending email messages with the purpose of enhancing a merchant's relationship with current or previous customers, encouraging customer loyalty and repeat business, acquiring new customers or convincing current customers to purchase something immediately, and sharing third-party ads."

EMAIL INTERACTION

Wikipedia defines email marketing as:

"The Interaction via email delivered computer to computer, device to device, or by using an email responding program, that involves the exchange of information, questions, answers, and feelings through the use of typed information. It can also include graphics, videos, audio files, or links to podcasts, websites, or social media."

In Selling in the Real World, email communication has the advantage of being able to create a written record between two or more people of the exchange of information regarding the product or service being offered for sale (or being considered for purchase).

Advantages of email include the ability to control the specific language being sent to potential customers for distribution at the same time. This initial email contact is designed to generate a response in people who would be interested in what you are selling. The success of this kind of email depends on your ability to find potential buyers based on the demographics and psychographics of the people who receive your email. This form of marketing is often called a "blast." Blasts go to a wide range of people hoping that you have chosen recipients who are most likely to respond because of a need you believe they have for your product or service.

Blasts should include enough to get them interested in the product or service but not so much that they decide to not read or respond to your presentation.

Disadvantages of email marketing involve the difficulty of finding appropriate recipients. Blasters commonly do searches of social media to find emails. Do note that using such emails runs the risk of being labeled as a spammer. Purchasing lists of emails without knowing if the emails were acquired with the knowledge and permission of the recipients of the email also runs the more real risk of falling into the realm of spamming.

YOUTUBE

Wikipedia says this about YouTube:

> "YouTube is an American online video-sharing platform and is the second most-visited website after Google Search. Users upload, view, rate, share, add to playlists, report, comment on videos, and subscribe to other users. Available content includes video clips, TV show clips, music videos, short and documentary films, audio recordings, movie trailers, live streams, video blogging, short original videos, and educational videos. Most content is generated and uploaded by individuals, but media corporations offer some of their material via YouTube as part of the YouTube partnership

program. Unregistered users can watch, but not upload videos on the site, while registered users can upload an unlimited number of videos and add comments.

"YouTube and selected creators earn advertising revenue from Google AdSense, a program that targets ads according to site content and audience. The vast majority of videos are free to view, but there are exceptions, including subscription-based premium channels, film rentals, and ad-free access to all content, including exclusive content commissioned from notable personalities."

Sales personnel may create videos to promote their products, explain usages and tips, and in general broadcast the benefits of their products and services. Some Sales people use YouTube to promote their own brand and become mini-celebrities who gather followers via subscription. These followers in turn promote the online sales person to their friends and followers. Sales personnel may also purchase ads to be placed in situations that are directly connected to their products and services in order to reach people who may be interested in buying from them.

Using the power of video and the permanence of YouTube channels, sales people can transfer the authority of expertise to themselves, their products and services, and to the organization for which they work.

BLOGGING

Wikipedia says this about Blogging:
"A blog — a truncation of 'weblog' — is a discussion or informational website published on the World Wide Web consisting of discrete, often informal diary-style text entries (posts). Posts are typically displayed in reverse chronological order, so that the most recent post appears first, at the top of the web page."

Originally a form of personal journaling or diarying, blogs today are sources of information generated by both individuals and companies. Sales professionals can create and maintain a blog as a source of information concerning their products and services as well as industry, corporate, governmental, and social happenings. Blogs can have members, subscribers, followers, or simply exist and function as randomly accessed websites.

The Sales Professional who blogs would do so to create the reputation of expertise, understanding, willingness to help, finding the correct solution to customer problems, and generally to keep their user base informed and updated. While blogging is not often thought of as a strong sales tool, the ability to cultivate and grow a blog can have huge, long-range benefits.

chapter six

Prospecting and Setting Initial Appointments

Prospecting is the process of looking for, and hopefully finding, new sales opportunities. In the larger sense, the whole world is available to you, filled with potential customers. In reality, you have to find the following small groups of people and companies who

1. Need your product or service
2. Are looking for your product or service
3. Are willing to consider your product or service

In reality, this is a world that is actually available for you to interact with.

So, how do you find the individuals who are in that world? You prospect. You can use any and all of the social and messaging media listed in the previous chapter, as well as your telephone, to reach out to your potential customers, your prospects. It all starts with an initial contact known as the cold call.

Cold calling consists of sending a generalized introduction to an unknown person in a company whom you have decided MIGHT be someone who SHOULD or COULD be a potential customer of your product or service. One of two things will happen next: there will be either an active response or there will be a passive silence.

In the active response situation, there are two options, positive or negative. In the positive scenario you move through a series of continuing contacts from the broad overview to the specific, ultimately resulting in an interaction that leads to a purchase. Your cold calling has achieved its purpose: interacting with someone who has the need, willingness, and authority to buy from you.

In the negative scenario, you are dealing with rejection. But even a "NO" doesn't necessarily mean "don't talk to me." It simply allows you to respond in a manner with could open the opportunity to continue to interact, or in which you can graciously invite further contact when the timing is better for the recipient of your cold call and which allows for keeping them updated on any changes in the product or service or notification of a sale.

No matter which level of rejection you encounter in response to your cold call, to be a successful sales person you need to not take rejection personally but to continue your cold calling with the next person, company, or prospecting media on your to do list.

Another type of prospecting is called Sales Leads by Referral. This is a process of acquiring leads as referrals from other customers or business partners. If you have plenty of good customers, this is a helpful source of new business. Because of The Law of Diminishing Returns (the same input returns less and less output), Sales Leads by Referral is a supplemental activity, not a primary one. So the successful sales rep realizes that this by itself cannot keep you at the level of positive results you need to get and remain successful. If sales people could fill their sales funnel simply by referral, then management could reduce compensation. Because referral is easy, pay may be low. Because prospecting is difficult, pay must be high.

I can recall a sales rep I once managed who believed he could become successful without putting in the necessary work of developing a strong sales funnel of potential customers by making cold calls. Because he did not have a strong sales funnel, his sales were down and he had no plan to improve his situation. When I asked him how he intended to gain new prospects and close business to become sales healthy, the rep replied that he would bird-dog leads. Bird-dogging is sales slang for Sales Leads by Referral. He was going to ask his client list for names of people THEY thought he could contact who MIGHT buy from him. Shortly after our conversation, I had the unpleasant task of terminating this person's relationship with the company — a euphemism that means that I had to fire him.

Keep in mind that sales is a numbers game. To fill your sales funnel, cold calls must be made. When I led the branch in sales for Xerox Northern Ohio, I averaged twenty cold calls (via telephone and in person) a day, coupled with two or three face-to-face meetings. According to your business plan, to be successful in sales at least fifteen cold calls a day must be made, along with one or two scheduled face-to-face appointments with potential customers. This is the only surefire method to build a sales territory. Every successful salesperson needs to build their territory, unless they inherit an already existing gravy patch. Even then, bad things happen. Cold calling is difficult but imperative.

Cold calling falls in one of two zones: conversational and messaging. Conversational cold calling is that in which both sides use more than their visual sense to interact and includes the telephone, in-person, and chatting. Messaging cold calling relies almost entirely on the visual, at least at the beginning of the process. Conversational marketing includes both social and messaging media such as Facebook, LinkedIn®, texting, and all typing-dependent systems.

Because of the differences in the two zones, there are two different ways to think about how to start — about what should be the first thing about you and your product with which the potential customer interacts.

CONVERSATIONAL COLD CALLING

1. Begin by identifying yourself, your company, and the reason for this interaction.

2. Ask a question of the prospect about their desires with regard to a future that includes the value-output of your product and service.

3. Continue questions and answers, about need and solutions.

4. Remain friendly, helpful, and at no time be combative.

5. Find ways to continue the course of this initial conversation for as long as it takes to get a response, either positive or negative, about the possibilities of your product being the solution they're in need of.

6. Always keep the door open for further contact.

MESSAGING COLD CALLING

1. Identify yourself and explain the reason for your cold call: what your product or service is or does.

2. Lead with a question that implies their desire, spoken or unspoken, for a solution to a problem you know or that you feel is reasonable for them to have.

3. When possible, include images that present a possible solution to the same problem.

4. If possible, include a request to discuss their specific needs for a solution.

5. Thank them for taking the time to read this and a tell them you are looking forward to continuing our conversation.

6. Keep this short and easy to read.

POTENTIAL INTRODUCTIONS

The following short statement identifies both yourself and your company. It provides a general benefit statement to gain this person's attention, offers an opportunity to meet you, and gives a choice of two different dates and times. Because your initial meeting will be brief — possibly as short as 30 minutes — they should be made to understand that no sales commitment on their part is required or even expected.

"Hello, Mr. O'Connor, I am Larry Sternlieb, of LSS. I am calling you because my organization has assisted ABC Company, a company I understand is similar to yours. What I would like to do is set up a brief meeting with you to discuss how LSS can benefit your company. Would you be available this Wednesday at 2:00 P.M. or Friday at 10:00 A.M. for that brief meeting?"

In a perfect world, Mr. O'Connor will say yes and you can set up ten or fifteen more appointments in a similar manner. However, in the real world, this does not occur very often. As you might guess this is where the selling actually begins. These are some of the responses you will hear from the Mr. O'Connors of the world. Don't be taken aback!

OVERCOMING OBJECTIONS

As you progress in your sales career, you will develop your own responses that work well for you. What works best in all situations, however, is to keep responses simple, quick, and to the point. And never argue!

> **Objection:** *"I'm not interested."*
> **Response:** *"Mr. O'Connor many people say the same thing during my initial call. But after I help them increase their productivity, they always thank me for my persistence.*

> **Objection:** *"I'm just too busy!"*
> **Response:** *"I'm sorry to call at such a busy time. When can I call back that will be more convenient?"*

Should Objector respond with: "I'm not sure," you will need to give him an alternate choice response such as, "Would you like me to call back next week or next month?" If you continue to get indefinite responses, you can most likely assume you are dealing with someone who is not interested but who is unable to say no. Sometimes these people really are not able to be more specific yet they, in fact, do have an interest in your product/service. You can either remove them from your calling list or put them at the end.

> **Objection:** *"I'm happy with my current vendor."*
> **Response:** *"What do you like about your current vendor? What do you dislike?"*

Once you know Mr. O'Connor's likes and dislikes, you'll have valuable information that can help you completely eliminate his objections and disarm his concerns.

After The Objector reveals his likes and dislikes of his current vendor, your response should be:

"Mr. O'Connor, I understand that you work with the Johnson and Smith Company. That's the very reason we should meet. I can explain how I can enhance those services with my product. Are you free this Friday at 2:00 P.M.?"

> **Objection:** *"I don't need it at this time."*
> **Response:** *"Mr. O'Connor that's exactly what ABC Compan said before I upgraded them. Now they tell me that they couldn't afford not to upgrade. I'd like to discuss these areas with you. Can we meet briefly on Thursday at 1:30 P.M.?"*

> **Objection:** *"I can't afford it."*
> **Response:** *"Mr. O'Connor I'm remembering how your competitor told me the same thing. After buying our product, their revenues have increased. If we met for just one-half hour, I will show you that you can't afford NOT to review my solution."*

> **Objection:** *"Business is slow."*
> **Response:** *"Mr. O'Connor that's the best time to review my solution. ABC Company implemented my solution at a slow period and now they are rapidly increasing business. Can we get together for a brief meeting tomorrow at 10:00 A.M.?"*

> **Objection:** *"Send me a brochure."*
> **Response:** *"Of course Mr. O'Connor, I'd be happy to provide written information. Since I'll be in your area next Monday, could I deliver it to you at 2:00 P.M..?"*

> **Objection:** *"Do you have a website I can review."*
> **Response:** *"Of course Mr. O'Connor, it's www.website.com. Can we schedule a meeting after you review it?"*

OTHER WAYS

Selling in the Real World is not a rigid, static set of ideas. It is a fluid and responsive system determined by the real world. What used to be true may no longer be. But sometimes, an old, no-longer-popular method of getting a sales meeting may work well. Here are two options you might consider.

UNSCHEDULED IN-PERSON VISIT

In-person cold calls were very common when I first began my sales career. Now it is more efficient to utilize electronic means to set appointments. Seemingly most front desk people, or receptionists, are not accustomed to interacting with sales people and will check with the person responsible to see what they should do or say when you walk in. This is potentially a good way for you to break through the impersonal though efficient methods we discussed earlier.

Here is an example of what might happen. Keep in mind that all such dialogs in "Selling in the Real World" are not to be used word-for-word but are merely examples of concepts that you can modify to fit your product, service, and personal style.

> **Salesperson:** "Good Morning. My name is Larry Sternlieb. I'd like to speak to Mr. O'Connor." (If you don't know his/ her name, ask for the General or Operational Manager, General Partner or President.)
>
> **Receptionist:** "Do you have an appointment?"
>
> **Salesperson:** "No, that's why I would like for you to tell him it will only take a few minutes of his time. Would you do that for me please?"
>
> **Receptionist:** "What company are you with?"
>
> **Salesperson:** "I am with LSS, here's my card."

Receptionist: "Are you selling something?"

Salesperson: "LSS handles a wide line of Training and Consulting Services. We have recently introduced a new system that we feel will greatly enhance your organization. I'd like to talk to him about it for a few minutes."

If after several interactions like this you haven't been able to secure your face-to-face meeting, make sure you have the appropriate name, phone number, and/or email for the person to whom you want to meet and say you'll get in touch with that person later. Then, depart with a smile and a thank you.

Geographical salespeople should more frequently utilize the in-person unscheduled cold call on small, closely held companies. This approach, however, might be inappropriate for a Major Account Salesperson requesting to visit a Senior Vice President, for example.

MAIL DELIVERY

What once was the standard and only method of delivering information, other than in person, is the mail. Today that includes the US Postal system as well as delivery companies such as FedEx.

Getting a letter or full-color postcard MIGHT cut through any barriers and get attention. See the list above about Messaging Cold Calling for things to include to get the attention of the people seeing your delivery.

Here is a sample letter good for mail delivery, overnight delivery, or even email. Once again, this is not intended to be used word-for-word. It is a starting point for you to create your own.

· ——————— · ——————— ·

100 Million Dollar Blvd.
New York, NY 12345

BETTER SALES TRAINING RESULTS IN BETTER PROFIT.
EVERY TIME.

Dear Mr. O'Connor,

As the owner of one of America's most recognized resellers of technical products, it is essential to not only maintain your valued customer base, but also to enhance it. It is our experience that when working with fine organizations such as Best Sales Corporation, your realized sales volumes can be made even more profitable with a little fine-tuning.

Our organization has assisted companies very similar to yours, such as ABC Corporation also located in NYC, and has notably increased their sales revenues by 20 percent. We can provide similar, top-notch, custom-tailored training to Best Sales Corporation.

A small investment of your time will show you how our organization can make you more organized, effective and profitable. I will be contacting your office on Tuesday to request an appointment at a mutually convenient time.

Thank you in advance for your consideration and interest.

Best regards,

Larry J. Sternlieb
President
LSS Corporation

· ——————— · ——————— ·

OTHER LEAD GENERATING METHODS

What we have discussed so far are all direct methods of prospecting. Here are some indirect methods. Generally, indirect means that you join organizations, participate in the community, and get yourself known as a connected, responsible, good person. With indirect methods, you are building your character, stature, and image.

- Civic organizations
- Business and social conferences
- Network marketing groups
- Write for publications: local, city, business, trade organizations
- Contribute to blogs
- Marketing sales leads and other computer intelligence reports
- Join social media groups that connect with your industry, product, or service

Leads can be acquired anywhere. Always have your business card available to exchange, or offer to forward your contact information.

MISCELLANEOUS FORMS

You should track all your appointments both scheduled and completed. An Appointment Scheduling Form is a gauge of how successful you have been in scheduling new appointments during a given week. Always try to reach your objectives of obtaining at least five new appointments per week. And, if you are lucky enough to fill this schedule with twenty new appointments, do take yourself out for lunch or dinner. You deserve it!

Also, there is an activity tracking form you can use if your work-provided software does not include one.

APPOINTMENT SCHEDULING FORM.

Sales Rep: _____ **Week Ending:** _____

	COMPANY NAME	PROSPECT NAME	APPOINTMENT DATE	TIME	PROSPECT REQUEST	COLD CALL IN PERSON	ON PHONE
1							
2							
3							
4							
5							
6							
7							
8							
9							
10							
11							
12							
13							
14							
15							

Please record all new appointments that have been scheduled. This report should not include appointments that were previously scheduled and that appeared on previous reports. Record all appointments that were scheduled during the course of this week even though the scheduled date and time may be in the future. This report will help determine how well you are doing in scheduling new appointments which are the lifeblood of your business.

NOTES

chapter seven

Qualifying: Turning Suspects into Prospects

A suspect in sales is not a potential perpetrator of a crime. A suspect in sales is an unqualified prospect, someone who — with effort on your part — might be turned from *not-interested-in-buying-from-you* to *considering-the-possibility-of-buying*.

The sales process begins with

1. Prospecting: looking for suspects
2. Setting appointments with suspects to discuss their needs
3. Qualifying: turning suspects into prospects through the process of questioning

Following are the qualifying questions which, when answered affirmatively, will usually qualify the person or organization as a prospect:

- Are you the decision-maker?
- Are you the person who signs the orders and checks?
- When are you going to make a decision on this project?
- Do you already have available funding for the project?
- Are you reviewing other vendors outside of our company?
- What is the formal decision-making process and are there others who will be involved?
- Does this project require a Board of Directors approval?
- Will this order go through the purchasing department?

The answers to those questions will tell you if you are dealing with the correct person within the company. Time spent on someone who cannot make the decision is time wasted. If you have chosen to make your presentation to the wrong person, you will either be turned away without meeting the decision-maker or you will have to repeat your entire sales presentation to the person who can give the okay. In an extreme situation, your job could be in danger. Most likely your direct supervisor included your forecast within his forecast to his supervisor. When your sale fails, his forecast takes a hit. Ultimately, that problem for him will fall on your shoulders. Too many forecasts based on the wrong person and you could be on your way out — both for not making the sale and for making your direct supervisor look bad. Upper management does not look kindly upon poor forecasting!

It is extremely important, then, to take the time to ask these qualifying questions. This is not the time to be timid. If your contact is a legitimate prospect, he will respect your questions and truthfully provide the necessary answers. And you will determine if he/she is the correct decision-maker or learn who is. If you get the runaround, end the process politely and leave. Don't waste your time and effort. As one of my respected direct managers once told me, don't chase ghosts.

It should always be your intention to work with the highest ranking decision-maker within the organization who has the responsibility for approving your sale. Lower level, frontline managers may be an enormous waste of your time. Many times, these individuals have personal, non-business-based reasons for not wanting to change vendors. These reasons include having a personal relationship with your competitor or being unwilling to involve himself and his staff in learning a new system or process. By considering your product or service, that manager could weaken his position in his company which may be based on being trained in the operation of your competitor's system.

In situations like this, the frontline manager may deal with you pleasantly and take your information but stop your sales progress dead in its tracks. Or he may even use you by requesting a competitive quotation or proposal that must be significantly less money than their current vendor, which is most likely your direct competitor.

After receiving your excellently-priced solution, that manager will then tell their current vendor to sharpen their pencil or lose that account to you. Your competitor will usually reduce their price to maintain that account.

This process of reducing your competitor's price will make that manager very attractive to his upper management since he will have saved his company large amounts of money — at your expense! Consequently, that manager could receive a pay raise or additional company stock options as a result of a fictitious project that he had no intention of facilitating. To avoid these kinds of problems, always sell to the highest-level person whose mission is to increase company capabilities as opposed to furthering their own, personal agenda.

How do you get to that person? You start by asking by the first person you have to interact with until you get the name and an appointment to talk to the decision-maker. If you get objections to making this happen, go back to page 85 and read how to deal with objections.

Your success in qualifying is determined by the questions you ask the suspect and the answers you get. Without knowing the affirmative answers to the following checklist, do not include that account in your sales funnel as a legitimate prospect.

QUALIFYING QUESTIONS YOU MUST ANSWER
A. Who makes the decisions?
  1. The main decision-maker is:
  2. Are others involved in making this decision?
  3. Does this decision require Board of Trustees approval?
  4. Does this decision require Purchasing Department approval?
  5. Have all layers of management agreed to purchase a new product or solution?

B. Do they have funding available?
  1. Has funding been established by the company?
  2. Has this company established an identified amount of money to be spent?
  3. Will funding be available for multiple years?
  4. Is leasing an option?
  5. Will a higher price eliminate competitors?
  6. Is there a Return on Investment (ROI) or Return on Equity (ROE) established by this organization?
  7. Is the company financially sound?

C. What is the time frame for this purchase?
1. Is there a compelling event causing this decision? If so, when and why?
2. Has a date for this decision been determined?
3. Has a predetermined installation date been determined?
4. Does this decision require immediate attention?
5. Does it make good business sense to proceed immediately?
6. Has a timeline involving a series of key steps in the sales cycle been determined?

D. Is the project definitely coming to fruition?
1. Have they stated and identified requirements?
2. Is there an absolute concrete need viewed by all management to proceed with this project?
3. Have all or at least most key decision-makers met with you?
4. Is there consensus on the project, its time frame, and available funding?
5. Do they require an on-site test demo, or benchmark?
6. Does the main decision-maker state that there is indeed a project?

E. Will they choose my solution over my competitor's?
1. Can I solve their need?
2. Does my product-offer satisfy the company's requirements?
3. Do I know all my competitors? Do I offer unique value?
4. Is there a preferred vendor? Is that vendor you?
5. Is your solution cost effective when compared to your competitors?
6. Am I well liked in the organization? Are there any hidden agendas?
7. Have I responded to all their requests and questions on a timely basis?
8. Do I have credibility with their management?

F. Is it Good Business?
1. Can I realize good long-term and short-term revenue streams?
2. Is this profitable business?
3. Can this account and application be referenced?
4. Is my solution a good fit in a selected SIC code or is there some technical risk to implement my offering?

These questions are usually asked during the first segment of your initial sales call with the company or as they become appropriate in the course of the sales process. Sometimes, especially with large major accounts, these qualifying questions can even be directed to the suspect during the initial appointment scheduling sequence. There are no shortcuts in qualifying a suspect into a prospect. You must know the answers to everything on this checklist or you will likely be wasting your valuable time.

Asking tough questions and getting the answers is the only way to fill your sales funnel with quality accounts and not just a quantity of suspect accounts.

NOTES

chapter eight

Strategizing, Organizing, and Planning for the Buying Decision

When I first began my sales career, I would contact a company's marketing department and request an annual report. If they mailed it to me, I had to wait a week. Often, I drove to the office and picked it up. Today, acquiring the information contained in a company's annual report is as easy as going to their website. Once you have the raw data, you want to learn as much as you can. Specifically, you'll want to know:

- Who are the corporate executives?
- What are their business objectives and mission statements?
- How do they make money, and have their revenues increased this year?
- Who was recently promoted and why?
- Who are their direct competitors? Have you ever called on their competitors?

Your goal in obtaining this information is to determine areas where their needs match up with your services. I call this a company's area of pain. If you are selling information services of some sort, for example, look for areas that could contain procedures that may cause bottlenecks or backups of information. These may cause corporate management to not receive data on a timely basis, creating delayed billings, delayed receivables, and possible inefficiencies in their organization.

You are looking for a situation in which time is needlessly consumed in order to determine what this loss of time or lack of efficiency is costing this company.

If your product and service can eliminate or reduce those areas of pain in a way that makes good business sense to you, then there's a reasonable chance it may make good business sense to your potential customer as well.

Make printed copies of the company's website information and highlight important areas. This will organize your focus before your scheduled appointment and greatly impress your soon-to-be client during your appointment.

This process of collecting important information prior to the initial face-to-face meeting can be enhanced by discovering the answers to questions on the Pre-Call Questionnaire. Knowing the answers to these questions can help you be selected as the vendor of choice by any prospective company. All of these areas of information collection should be addressed in your sales call.

PRE-CALL QUESTIONNAIRE

- What is the company profile?
- What do they manufacture?
- What products or service do they manufacture or provide?
- What is their mission statement?
- What is their operating philosophy?
- Who are the corporate executives?
- Who are their direct competitors?
- What are the current industry trends?
- How are their financial situations?
- Is business on an up swing or downturn? Why?
- When were revenues good?
- When were revenues not so good?

There's no doubt that it's easier to wing an initial meeting than to spend the time it would require to research the answers to all these questions for each and every qualified sales call you go on — but it's not better. Knowledge increases professionalism; lack of knowledge reduces it. The more you know about a company, the better prepared you are to answer their objections and involve yourself in the process.

Your goal in becoming a successful salesperson and in turning a suspect into a prospect is to make clients look to you as the person who is the expert in solving their problems. Your lack of preparation will be perceived by the potential client as a lack of professionalism and diminish their belief in your ability to solve their problems.

The potential customer might interpret an unprofessional attitude as avaricious and assume the salesperson is just trying to collect a commission, and not help the organization be more successful. When a decision-maker observes that attitude, they may wonder why they are wasting time with someone who wasn't willing to take the time to get to know them.

Being well versed in all pertinent aspects of the prospective company is the mechanism by which your potential client will recognize your credibility and value the suggestions you offer to solve their problems. Being recognized as the expert in solving their problems is crucial to the process of differentiating yourself from your competitors.

Sales professionals must earn the right to ask for a company's business at the point of closing the deal. If you do a thorough job from the very beginning of the sales process, asking for the business at the end is an easy, almost automatic, result. Moreover, if you do a very good job, your potential client may not even seriously consider your competition as a credible option.

This initial information call will lead you into detailed discussions that can uncover areas of pain. When you finally are in front of your suspect, asking fact-finding questions will help create a feeling of partnership in solving the potential client's problems. Pay close attention to answers because if followed up correctly, they will lead you directly into what the client considers to be his/her area of concern. Once you know that, you can structure the way in which your products and services can solve their problems and reduce or eliminate their pain.

INFORMATION GATHERING SALESCALL

"Mr. O'Connor, I have observed from your website that your overall revenues of the domestic sale of laptop computers decreased last year. I am curious if you know why that is?"

— or —

"Mr. O'Connor, I would like to congratulate you on your promotion to Vice-President of Sales and Marketing. Obviously, you have worked very hard and been very focused. To what do you attribute your success? What are your new responsibilities?"

— or —

"Mr. O'Connor how has your current vendor been handling these areas for your company? Have you been satisfied with their efforts?"

Here is an example of a possible dialog between the salesperson and prospect.

Salesperson: *"Mr. O'Connor, I see your overseas computer systems utilize router-based technology. Do you acquire accurate, timely information utilizing this process?"*

O'Connor: *"Well not really. Sometimes our data is retrieved one or even two days late."*

Salesperson: *"What type of problems could this create for you?"*

O'Connor: *"We may not be very rapid in our response to international customer order fulfillment. And, to be honest, sometimes our receivable revenue can be late in its arrival."*

Salesperson: *"Mr. O'Connor that sounds like a pressing problem. What do you think your company could lose in revenues if your customer cancels an order due to lack of timelines? What monies could you be losing by not receiving your monies sooner, thereby depositing those funds into an account one or two days sooner?"*

O'Connor: *"That could be significant. Maybe hundreds of thousands, or even millions of dollars for our larger customers."*

By asking fact-finding questions, you will receive answers which will allow you to create at least two legitimate reasons for an organization to buy your services or product. This process will be discussed in greater detail in the next chapter.

Before you make your initial sales call, spend time researching everything you can about the company. From that information, create a written list of questions to ask during the initial sales meeting. Take your highlighted web pages with you and use them for reference. Listen to the answers you get to your questions in order to discover the client's area of pain. Then solve his problems using your products and services.

Following this process will give you the edge you need to win every opportunity you choose to compete for.

If you want to be a successful salesperson, you have to repeatedly and consistently follow a system that works. You'll never be a winner if you look for short cuts.

NOTES

chapter nine

Selling Obstacles
in the Twenty-First Century

In the last century, selling seemed much less complicated. Executive decision-makers had secretaries to screen their calls. It was considered an art form for salespeople to "dazzle" call screeners and get through to the decision-maker. Today voice mail, email, or texting has replaced the human screener. As a result, potential clients spend less time with sales personnel. At the same time that downsizing has required more work from each employee, sales companies may have created more products and services to sell. Thus, fewer and fewer clients spend less and less time reviewing all the options available to them.

The business environment, too, has been affected and swings wildly from optimism to hesitancy. Threats of terrorism, rising costs of business due to government regulations, inflation, resultant increases in energy costs, the loss of mid-level jobs, and the swing to working from home have all combined to make selling in the real world far more difficult than it was at the end of the last century.

Resourceful sales personnel see these seemingly negative situations not as insurmountable obstacles but rather as an opportunity to become one of only a few sales people overcoming them and gaining access to today's decision-makers.

VOICE MAIL

Like it or not, voice mail has replaced the call-screener in a large number of organizations. Like many, I initially disliked this isolating, electronic mechanism, devoid of human contact. Once I realized that no matter what I thought or felt about voice mail that it was here to stay, I began to see it as not something to avoid but rather as something to be used and taken advantage of.

It's common knowledge that the number of voice mail messages returned compared to the number of voice messages left is often quite low. However, I wonder if that percentage is actually any lower than the percentage of phone calls or cold calls that resulted in immediate contact with the decision-maker. In the old days of call screeners, successful sales personnel developed skills and systems to circumvent call screeners. Today, successful sales personnel are creating the same successful circumvention to voice mail.

These methods include, but are not limited to:

1. CREATE CURIOSITY

It is a natural human condition to wonder how someone knows something about us, what they know, and what it means. Since you will have done (or should have done) research on each of your qualified potential clients before you contact them, use that knowledge in an intriguing, curiosity-creating way.

> *"Mr. O'Connor, this is Larry Sternlieb of LSS. I recently became aware that you are reviewing some of your business processes. I would like to discuss several ways in which we can help improve your results. Please call me at ____ ."*

2. CREATE VALUE

Phone calls to your home from people asking you to take a survey are bothersome, aren't they? Absolutely. The same can be said for phone calls to decision-makers – unless those calls promise to add value. The successful sales person will position himself to improve the potential customer's current situation or to create a solution to problem they are currently experiencing. When we add value, we increase the chances for dialog.

"Mr. O'Connor, this is Larry Sternlieb of LSS. I have a concept that we have used successfully with one of your strongest competitors, ABC Corp, to turn more suspects into prospects and generate a larger sales ticket. I'd like to tell you how it works. Please call me at _____ ."

3. REFERENCE CONTACTS

We all like to be connected. When we know someone in common with someone else, we feel more comfortable. It's as close to knowing a stranger as one can be. The level of person we know in common also defines our relative status in life. So, if you can truthfully use a person's name or recommendation, it can open doors for you. Note that the catch is truthfully. If you fudge the relationship, that fact will become known and your credibility will be reduced to zero. Worse than zero, you could become the subject of negative discussion amongst the original potential client and his/her circle of influence. No one needs to create additional obstacles to selling in the real world. You have enough already.

"Mr. O'Connor, while attending a recent meeting at which Sam Christopher spoke, I believe he's a member of your board, I discovered you are reviewing your business processes. I am certain I can be of help. Please call me at _____ ."

4. IMPLY FEAR

There are two motivators in life: fear and reward. Fear is the stronger motivator and gets our attention quicker. In business, fear is rampant. There is the fear of losing our job, losing money, losing clients, losing prestige, losing reputation, losing status, and generally just losing out. If a decision-maker feels that returning your call may be an effective form of damage control, that call is likely to be made.

"Mr. O'Connor, I understand that your Board Chairman, John Johnston, has recently given a corporate directive requiring greater accountability for more detailed budget spending. I have some information that will help you achieve the level of accountability that Chairman Johnston is looking for. Please call me at _____ ."

Each of these techniques is designed to get the attention of the decision-maker and encourage him/her to call you back, nothing more, nothing less. A returned phone call means you have discovered how to use voice mail as your ally, not your enemy.

EMAIL

Email is usually less of an obstacle than voice mail. Many individuals in companies rely solely on electronic communication — email or text messaging. When email is required, suggested, or necessary, there are a few things to keep in mind to ensure the most effective use of this technology.

Unlike voice mail, email is visual and thus requires extra care on the sender's part. That is, you must be sure to write in complete sentences and use acceptable grammar. Spell checking is required but does not eliminate the absolute necessity for proof reading a printed hard copy.

You must make certain that your phraseology is persuasive yet precise. You must think through carefully what you say and the way in which you say it. While voice mails are routinely erased, emails are routinely saved in files dedicated to the topic at hand. Your email is no longer a fleeting message suggesting a return phone call. Your email is now the first tangible representation of you, your product, and your company.

Not only do emails tend to have a long life, they have a potentially long reach. Because of the ease of the technology, your email is easily forwarded to your prospect's peers, superiors, and even your competition to be used as an incentive to improve their offer over yours. Therefore, never write anything you aren't willing to stand behind in public.

The style of your emails can and should follow the style of voice mails detailed earlier. They should create interest and curiosity, create value, refer to important contacts, and/or imply fear. As in voice mail messaging, your use of emails has one goal and one goal only: to elicit a response from your potential client.

Emails are written products and as such they will follow the rules of letter writing used much more extensively in the last century. Quickly identify who you are, use the attention getting format you've chosen (interest, curiosity, value, reference, fear) within the first several sentences, and make sure the recipient's next step is clearly delineated – to call you back because of the format chosen.

In addition to being an introductory, attention-getting media, email is a powerful and immediate thank you for a face-to-face meeting, phone conversation, or whatever has transpired. In addition to the thank you, include in your follow-up email a clear-but-subtle reference to your goal, that is, the sale of your product and/or service.

TEXTING/INSTANT MESSAGING

If you have their cell number, and you have their permission to send texts to them, this is the most efficient, direct, and effective method of communicating with customers. The same format — phrasing and methods — as described above in email and voice mail applies in texting. Be professional in your delivery. Until you have an informal business relationship, use standard spellings and sentences as you would in emails.

It is true, however, that in texting, you can become more informal in your contact once you and the client are comfortable with each other. This level of communication improves your opportunities for increased sales — people buy from people they know and trust.

In spite of its immediate and powerful communication systems, the Twenty-First Century can be a cold and impersonal environment in which to be a sales person, especially if one gets caught up in the gadgetry. The goal of voice mail, email, and cell phones — and whatever comes next — is the same as it has been for thousands of years – to arrange a direct or virtual face-to-face meeting with your potential client. The dynamic of one-to-one interactions is still the most effective method for selling products and services. The foundation of selling is basic to human existence – people buy from people. And nobody wants to be sold, they want to choose to buy. No amount of technology can alter this basic tenet of Selling in the Real World.

FIRST IMPRESSIONS LAST

A good and lasting first impression is important.

Dress appropriately. Moderate, not trendy, business attire
is usually the rule of thumb for an initial meeting. Since you
only have one chance to make a first impression, make it a
professional one.

Other essential behavioral elements include:
- Making good eye contact
- Displaying an air of
  confidence
- Being direct, but friendly.

chapter ten

Structuring the Initial Sales Call

Once you have done the research and have a relatively good understanding of your client's business, you are ready to structure the initial sales call. The initial sales call is not usually the key appointment with the key decision-makers. It is the first contact with an individual from the targeted account who might:

- Provide information and intelligence regarding the opportunity for securing business from this account.
- Become a supporter, sales coach, or an inside salesperson for your product and/or services.
- Set up the next step involving a high level executive sales presentation, including their decision-makers.

If you are calling on a very small organization, a two or three person office for example, it is possible your executive presentation or demonstration will be with this same individual. In a situation like that, it is even possible that your initial sales call could slide into a key appointment and you might be fortunate enough to close the sale. Because one-call closes sometimes do occur, the successful salesperson should always have blank order forms available at all times.

With your objectives in mind and with a wide array of documentation online or in hand — such as charts, reference material, website information — you are now prepared to make your initial sales call.

Almost.

If this is an on-site meeting, when you arrive and if it seems appropriate, you may ask the sales screen, if there one (usually a receptionist) some of the qualifying questions that were covered in the previous chapter. A successful salesperson is always gathering information.

When meeting for the first time with, say Mr. Hopkins, be friendly. Spend the first few minutes establishing rapport by discussing something other than your sales pitch. This can be an excellent approach to begin your conversation, since it is non-pressuring, friendly, and might contain a possible segue to your sales call. Local current events (nonpolitical and nonreligious) might be a good topic. Or if your meeting is in person, you might get a clue for a topic from the items on his desk or wall. You may discover, for example, that Mr. Hopkins recently participated in a golf (or other sports) tournament and has a memento of his participation.

Make sure the topic of conversation centers on your potential client and not on you. After a few minutes of conversation, gently guide Mr. Hopkins into your sales meeting. The process should proceed smoothly making Mr. Hopkins feel completely at ease. This approach will help you break the ice and begin steering your potential client toward a favorable conclusion.

Once you have broken the ice, present the list of questions you have prepared. Do this before any product presentation is delivered!

The answers you receive will allow you to discover what's important to your client. You may even discover their area of pain, which will allow you to sell to a specific problem solution and not just deliver a general, unfocused presentation involving your product features and services. Average, or unsuccessful salespeople, often carry on a discussion that does not address the needs or interest of the potential client. To avoid this, ask your researched questions first to determine your client's areas of interest.

If you discuss only your product and its price, you will be seen as a seller of commodities. But if you can help your prospect visualize how you can help solve his problems, you will be seen as a value-added partner, a person who understands him, his company, and his business objectives. By asking qualifying questions of the prospect first, you will create the differentiating factor that will separate your organization from your competition.

Following your rapport-establishing conversation, your introduction to the reason for your meeting could go something like this. (Remember, the dialogs in this book should not be used word for word. They are concepts from which you should create a presentation that fits you, your personality, and your company's culture.

"Mr. Hopkins, I am Larry Sternlieb, President of LSS. I implement advanced learning systems to increase sales productivity. My purpose for meeting with you today is to see if I can provide the same type of value to you that I have provided for ABC Corporation. But first I would like to ask you a few questions so that I may better understand your operation. Could we spend a few moments so that I may discover your specific needs?"

Thus far, your conversation has included these elements:
- Rapport building
- Formal introduction
- Benefit or positioning statement
- Objective or purpose of meeting
- Presentation of advantages and possible references
- Permission to engage in the sales process
- Agreement by the prospect to allow you to ask questions

It is important to note that this is the first of many agreements necessary to win business. By allowing you to proceed, your prospect psychologically has begun the process of buying from you. Every time your prospect says yes, even to affirm the spelling of his name, he is affirming the buying signals that can domino into a sale for you.

During the questioning process, allow your prospect to do most of the talking. The ratio should be about 25% your questions and 75% their answers. Allowing your prospect to talk gives him the opportunity to reveal the information you will need to build your case for the sale of your products or services.

Questions should be both direct and indirect, or open-ended.

Direct questions begin with the words what, who, where, and when. An example of a direct question may be:
"What are your budgeted dollars for this project?"

Indirect questions begin with the words how and why.
An example of an indirect question may be:
"How would lack of timeliness to customer response cause loss of business?"

The direct question requires the prospect to recall information and provides you with facts.

The indirect question allows the prospect to relax and brainstorm regarding his needs and provides you with ideas and insight into his areas of pain and your potential path to complete the selling process.

An additional by-product of an indirect question is that, by telling you his problems, the prospect may begin to recognize for himself the need for your deliverable product or service. Your description of how your product or service will be able to help will then be seen as the logical decision, one he's already begun to accept. Helping a prospect come to this conclusion is an art form that most very successful salespersons have mastered. It is always a slow process and is never forced.

At the end of the questioning period, and using the prospect's own words and terminologies, restate his thoughts identifying critical issues and shortcomings with regard to his operation. Make sure you repeat language that addresses his general business type.

The following sample dialogue can be used as a guideline:
"Mr. Hopkins, you said your international division has slow turnaround for product delivery, especially in Europe. This allows other companies to capture some of your existing business from your customers. Is this a growing problem for your company?"

"Yes, definitely. My job is to fix this problem. How can you help me?"

Not only have you gained Mr. Hopkins's interest, but you've also created the vision that your delivered solution will help fix his problem. You have isolated Mr. Hopkins's areas of need or pain by using your prepared questions, the information collected from his website, and the situational questions you asked during this initial sales call.

The next step is to restate his areas of need, support those areas of pain, and participate in a joint solution necessary to fix his problems.

Once again, gain agreement with Mr. Hopkins and continue to qualify his needs:

"Mr. Hopkins, our software upgrade will allow you to immediately monitor your customers throughout the world. And I stress the word 'immediately,' Mr. Hopkins. This way, your company can instantaneously respond to your customers' needs, including shipping products in a timelier manner. Would that help eliminate your loss of business to XYZ Company?"

"Of course it would! Yes, that would do it."

Now is the appropriate time to ask all qualifying questions that will help you discover who the ultimate decision-maker is and if there is the possibility of completing this sale. You must continue to qualify this sales opportunity with every individual with whom you speak in this company. By doing so, you will gain consensus and consistency regarding you, your product or services, and how best to proceed to complete the sale. If most everyone, especially the top management, agrees on what is required and when it must be implemented, then you have thoroughly qualified this opportunity.

Your goal during the initial contact with this account is to:
- Establish their needs
- Identify the areas of pain in the organization
- Uncover who will make the decision to buy your product or service solution
- Set up the next steps in the sales process.

Always close for the order to be concluded or close for the next appointment. Never walk away without a definable next step. Usually, the next step will be into an executive sales presentation to the main decision-makers. It would be ideal if the individual you have just meet with in the initial sales call serves as your sponsor or sales coach to help assist your continued sales efforts. To be effective in that role, this person must see your solution as the best method to solve the company's problems and enhance productivity. He or she must also feel that if your product or service can improve productivity, then his or her problems can be eliminated. And, as a result of your solution being successful, he or she may be promoted directly due to having introduced or championed your solution.

Your goal is to help him/her see your relationship as a partnership, a partnership that will help everyone involved, especially him or her. The establishment of such a partnership will set you apart from your competition and create a value-added relationship that cannot be duplicated by your competition.

During my career, I have personally directly sold to CEOs of Fortune 500 corporations.

I often paid to go to black tie events, like the Cleveland Opera and the Cleveland Orchestra. These events are always attended by the CEOs of leading organizations in the community, along with their spouses. At one of these events, I wound up having a long talk with the CEO of one of the Fortune 500 organizations who was using of one of the Big Four accounting firms, a competitor of mine at the time. At the end of our conversation, he and his wife decided to invite me to attend the after party at his house. I was surprised to notice that one of people there was that competitor of mine.

During the party, the CEO surprised my by telling me he had decided to award me a project he had intended to give to my competitor.

This may not be a standard way of breaking into this level of account but it does happen.

When you're fishing for bass, you have to go to a pond that has bass in it. CEOs tend to gather socially in certain places for specific events. If you have a legitimate opportunity to attend one of these events, you should consider doing so and presenting your self in your best light. If you are NOT pushing for business when you meet these people, but are relating well, you might be considered the kind of person that a CEO is comfortable with and then, doors may open. They may not immediately — or perhaps ever — but you will have established yourself as a player in the mind of someone who could become a strong supporter farther down the road of your career.

A CEO like that can really open doors for you if he likes who you are and how you present yourself. Of course, if you are awarded a sale as a result, you will have to perform consistently at the highest level to keep in good standing.

But, if you are professional, you can do that.

NOTES

chapter eleven

Engaging the Prospect

One of the most difficult things that people have to do is listen. Listening, really hearing what someone else is saying, is difficult work. It can also seem boring and tiresome. But as mind-numbing as it may feel, listening well is the single-most important requirement to successful selling in the real world.

Every year, while the world grows up with faster and faster electronic sources of information and relaxation, the unintended consequence is that we are developing limited attention spans. If we don't get information quickly, we lose interest. Following the dialog and natural byplay of a conversation is difficult, if not impossible.

In earlier times, the number one method for the dissemination of information was talking to people, either one-on-one or in public speeches and presentations. It was a process of telling stories and of listening to them. Sales people who grew up in that era had no problem being able to listen to what their potential customers were telling them and then using that information to create solutions for the client's problems.

In spite of the changes in cultural expectations and realities, today's requirements to be successful in sales are exactly the same as they've always been: listen to the client, hear what they're saying, and use what's been heard to create solutions to their problems for which they are willing to pay.

The difficulty for today's sales person, then, is not in knowing what to do, the difficultly is in listening to the client. The difficulty is in knowing what to ask. The difficulty is in creating one of the most common of interpersonal events – a conversation.

Conversation between two strangers is always enhanced when one of the people involved asks questions. We are always willing to answer questions, especially when they are about us or things we know and care about. We are always reluctant to give out information for which there has been no request. We realize that kind of talking on our part gives away our innermost thoughts, so we avoid it. When the other person asks questions that elicit that same information, however, we are more than willing to tell them the same exact same thing we were reluctant to share unasked. Questions lead to conversation and conversation leads to gathering the information critical to the sales process.

So, how does one ask information-producing questions that are conversational and not threatening? The key is to never ask questions that can be answered with yes or no. Questions should always ask how and why. These kinds of questions are called 'open-ended.'

> *"Mr. O'Connor, how is the international aspect of your business going this year?"*

Following a question like this, pause, and listen to the answer. Follow up with another open-ended question that connects to the information just provided.

> *"That doesn't sound good. Why do you think that's happening?"*
> — or —
> *"That's great! What do you think is causing that to occur?"*

Once you have engaged the prospect with open-ended questions, you may proceed to questions that are designed to gain trust, increase rapport, or even set your first scheduled appointment. Keep these questions low-key and non-confrontational.

It might seem silly to tell you to keep these questions non-confrontational but not long ago confrontational selling approaches were quite common. These approaches utilized multiple levels of probing with challenging questions. In that time frame, I personally found great success with that style of selling, producing the most sales for three consecutive years for Xerox Cleveland.

After 9/11, the confrontational approach began to fade from popularity. Many corporate executives found the approach too forward, too challenging. They turned themselves off in its presence and simply shut down. When confrontational selling began to fade, the favored selling style once again returned to the conversational approach of the early Twentieth Century.

The conversation between you and potential clients should be perceived by the client as having or adding value. He or she must believe that you understand their problems well enough that your proposed solutions will actually solve, eliminate, or improve their problem. They must believe that you can enhance their business and that your products/ services will, without a doubt, show them a noticeable, significant, and/or immediate return on their investment.

Be careful to not present your organization or yourself too aggressively. Pushing your potential client will most likely result in you getting pushed right out the door and out of contention for the sale of your products/services. Enthusiasm is great — being pushy is not.

ELEVATOR PITCH

The term 'elevator pitch' refers to a description of what you do that is so short and to the point that it can be successfully delivered and understood during the space of a short elevator ride. In reality, your elevator pitch may change from client to client depending on their specific needs compared to the wide variety of solutions you may be capable of delivering. You will need to create a specific elevator pitch for each and every client. The content of your pitches will come directly from the conversations you have with a potential client.

As you pursue your conversations, you will acquire more and varied information about them, their problems, desires, experiences, thoughts, likes, and dislikes. The more you discover about them and their problems, the more benefit you can offer, the more value you will be able to add, and the more likely they will be to be interested in listening to your solutions. Each time you gather new information concerning needs, problems, and pain, your elevator pitch should change to reflect that added information. As your elevator pitch becomes refined, so does your solution to the problems. Therefore, with sufficient conversation you should be able to focus your elevator pitch to an increasingly accurate description of your ability to solve their problems and encourage further discussion that will ultimately lead to the sale.

One pitfall that overzealous sales personnel need to avoid is the temptation to over-promise the delivery of products and services. In essence, such promises are false and will ultimately lead to the creation of a negative description of you within the industry and worse, within your marketplace. Excellent sales personnel become true business partners who uncover problems and supply solutions that work. Keep in mind that every potential client has different reasons to buy. To be successful, your conversations must uncover the strongest ones. Your ever-changing elevator pitch must reflect that understanding.

Despite the differing particulars, each client will be interested to some degree in cost-saving and revenue-increasing solutions.

Your pitches should reflect those needs and contain three elements:
1. Restatement of Customer Concern
2. Positive General Benefit Statement or Resolution of Negative Circumstances
3. Conversational Hook.

Restate Customer Concern:
"Mr. O'Connor, you indicated that this new investment must be easy to use and eliminate unnecessary mistakes which you are currently experiencing."

Positive General Benefit Statement:
"Well, Mr. O'Connor, LSS will provide the very system that will help your organization achieve the aggressive goals management desires."

Conversational Hook:
"Could I interest you in that solution?"

Restate Customer Concern:
"Mr. O'Connor, you said your organization desperately needs help with customer relations."

Resolution of Negative Circumstances:
> *"I have a solution that specifically addresses your needs. LSS.*
> *will provide you with a customer service model that will be unparalleled in your industry and will bring customer relations up to the level you envision, and beyond."*

Conversational Hook:
> *"May I interest you in that solution?"*

Negative Circumstances should never be construed as the creation of fear within your customer. While implying fear is recommended as one of the elements that can be used within voice mail or email to generate a phone call, the creation of fear as a long-term selling element is still a negative reality. Once you leave the potential client's office, fear begins to wear off, much like Novocaine, leaving a distasteful sensation in the potential client. Forcing or threatening a prospect to agree with your solution likewise can create ill will which increases in effect once you leave. Presenting benefits of your solution as opposed to focusing on the negative or different realities of your competition's solution is always the best thing to do.

When you degrade the competition, several things happen, none of them good.

1. Focusing on the competition takes the client's mind off of you and your solution. It's never a good idea to have people think about things that don't concern you and your solution.
2. People who demean others are soon known as being negative. No matter how isolated you think you might be from your competition, you soon discover it's a small world. When you degrade, the person most negatively affected is not them, it's you.

Because we live in such a small universe, you never know when you might find yourself working for the very competition which you are currently degrading. Trying then to sell their solution to a vendor on whom you have once called will not be easy. In fact, you most likely will be viewed as being insincere and untrustworthy, without integrity or credibility.

Without these attributes, your career in sales may never develop. You must be known for your trust, concern, believability, and your willingness to go the extra mile. Something as simple as degrading your competition instead of promoting the positive aspects of your own solution could negatively and irreversibly impact your sales career.

The ease of speaking negatively is never worth the possible negative results.

Rather than forcing decisions on your clients, let them come to their own conclusion. The same conclusion you would choose for them if the decision were your own.

> **Salesperson:** *"Mr. O'Connor, how could you see my solution creating value and solving your problems?*

> **O'Connor:** *"Larry, I can see that your solution would probably improve our prospecting and the customer presentations our sales force would be making. I think we'd even do a better job of closing with your system. I think customer service would be enhanced if we could make sure it works in the steel industry as you say it will."*

At this point, you will assure the client that their specific needs and requirements will be built into your solution and that what they are getting from you is a customized solution that speaks directly to their problems. By involving your customer in the solution, he or she will not feel manipulated into purchasing a one-size-fits-all solution. Win-win will be the order of the day.

Selling in the real world requires a conversational approach that engages the prospect and elicits information that goes directly to creating the solution for their problems. From the information you acquire, you will create an ever-changing elevator pitch that will continue to assure your potential client that your solution is the one they seek. Asking open-ended questions focused on their understanding of your solution will create a scenario in which the potential client begins to convince himself of the value of your solution. Avoiding direct and challenging questions will allow you to create a higher level of rapport, building trust and confidence in you and your solution. Make certain that all your solutions add value and speak directly to costs and benefits.

Conversations allow you to:
- Obtain information by uncovering needs
- Create an ever-evolving precise elevator pitch for the specific client and product
- Establish personal value to the client
- Develop customized solutions

Your ability to develop and use thought provoking questions will not only generate the information you desire, it will help you establish yourself as a trustworthy, credible salesperson with a high degree of integrity.

HELPING THEIR MANAGEMENT BUY YOUR SOLUTION

Always create and maintain your company's value proposition. Your company's proposal should provide leading-edge solutions that the client's executive team could have helped visualize. By their input into that process, their top management can buy into your solution and that solution will be embraced by everyone. If your solution is effective, you will solidify those executives with job security and safety. Moreover, they may even receive pay raises or promotions and increased power because of your solution.

NOTES

chapter twelve

The Sales or Product Presentation

The sales or product presentation can truly be considered 'show-time' The quality of your performance in front of the main decision-makers almost always determines whether you make or break a sale. Just as any performer has to rehearse before taking the stage, you too, have to be ready to perform.

Prior to the Sales or Product Presentation, you may have had numerous meetings with other members of ABC Corporation like Mr. Hopkins, which should have produced a formidable collection of data about this company. There should be no guess work now. You should know what it will take to close the deal.

As a result of your meetings and researching their website, you know who the decision-makers are, you understand their personalities, you know what their requirements are and even some of their private agendas. Using this information, create major points of need for the company using the customer's own terminologies. Present that in a format that can be displayed on a computer or a monitor either remotely or in person. Keep in mind that while you have done significant research and gained great insight into your prospect's company, you can never know everything. Therefore, it is always important to ask the main decision-makers if you have missed any other areas of interest, need or general criteria that they recognize as being essential for the success of their company.

Your direct supervisor, as well as others in your organization, should have input on your presentation. After reviewing and finalizing your presentation, invite the appropriate coworkers within your company to be part of your presentation team. To further impress your prospect and show them you are serious about obtaining their business, try to match the members of your team to the corresponding members of their team. If your client's audience includes a Senior Vice President, then it would be reasonable for you to include the Senior Vice President representing your company. Bringing a full team to the Executive Sales Presentation shows the prospect that your company will do whatever it takes to not only obtain their business, but to support them after the sale.

The personality mix attending the presentation must be compatible, however. If ABC's company Senior VP has a strong-willed, 'Type A' personality, then it would not be recommendable to invite your company's Senior Vice President if he, too, has the same type of personality. In this case, you may have matched the positions correctly but the resultant personal dynamics could negate your solution from being selected. Put a lot of thought into who you invite to your executive presentation to make sure there will be no personality clashes.

Usually, you will introduce the members on your sales team as being the specific individuals who will support that account once the sale is completed with you being the first point of contact at your company, the quarterback of the team, if you will. During this presentation, you will coordinate who presents which aspect and when this will occur. Each member of your team should deliver the part of the presentation with which he or she is most familiar. Prepare an itinerary that summarizes the needs you have identified and specifies the areas to be discussed. Provide references of accounts that have benefited from a very similar solution, preferably in the same industry as the prospect.

After you introduce your team members, ask that each member of your client's team introduce themselves and their position in the company and describe their specific objectives or expected outcomes of your meeting. Make sure to reaffirm those objectives. As a result of this process, there will likely be new, previously unknown objectives that will surface. During the presentation, your team must address all of the objectives stated, both new and previously known. You can see it is of the utmost importance to uncover as many objectives as possible prior to your sales team's presentation so that your team members can prepare themselves to best address those objectives, needs, concerns, or areas of pain.

Remember to restate the objectives and/or concerns they have presented, then ask if they have any more to add. Uncovering objections is critical to the sales process. An objection stated is no longer an objection, it is now a concern that can now be answered and be eliminated. Encouraging your prospect to talk about objections allows you to satisfy all their requirements and thus gain agreement for your solution.

If there are objectives and concerns that you can't meet, now is the time to deal with them. We're not talking about 'show-stoppers' here, because your intense due diligence would have uncovered those long ago, forcing you to decide if it was worth your time to present to this client or not. What we're talking about are the minor differences that often exist between desired specs and available specs. Often your competition will have the same or similar discrepancies between their product and the client's requested specs, forcing the client's buying decision to be based on other criteria entirely. For example if they spec 12 oogles per framitz and your equipment can only deliver 10, you need to ask them directly if that will be problem.

If they say no, you can consider that concern dealt with and continue on with the meeting. If they tell you that 10 oogles per framitz will be a problem, the selling process is not necessarily ended. You tell them that all solutions are not equal and they will have to evaluate all the pluses and minuses of your solution as well as the pluses and minuses of any competitor's solutions and decide which choice, overall, will be best for them. Then continue on as if you had met their objection for, indeed, you have!

Because your Vice President is well versed in your company's products and services, he is a logical choice to deliver the corporate capabilities portion of the presentation. That your Vice President will spend his valuable time addressing your prospect should be impressive to the prospect's team.

Because it is politically correct never to interrupt a superior (especially if he or she is two or three levels above you in authority), as a sales team, discuss in advance who will answer which questions that will most likely arise. Preparing and rehearsing most every element of your entire approach to this meeting will ensure that your sales team is seen by the prospect as one complete, highly-qualified entity.

After your Vice President has reviewed his points, it is customary for a technical engineer or industry expert to review your solutions. A solution with several options is always to be desired. For example, one solution may be very elaborate and most probably is the best overall answer to your client's areas of need. Unfortunately, the solution may exceed the cost allocations for their project.

The resourceful sales professional will have another, less expensive option which may satisfy both their requirements and their budget. Having more than one alternative in anticipation of the client's possible objections offers you the best opportunity to close the deal.

If your higher priced solution is clearly the best choice for the customer, there are ways to make the sale happen, even if your solution is apparently beyond their cost constraints. For example, the project could be delivered in phases over a multi-year timeframe. This way the organization may be able to utilize multiple years of budgeted monies rather than one, specific annual allotment allowing the client to immediately realize the best solution for their requirements and yet stay within their budget.

Another option might be leasing. Leasing can provide the full expenditure of monies for a complete installation of your product or service while allowing the prospect as many as five years in which to pay. Best of all, your prospect may be able to depreciate the interest and much of the balance of monies paid for your solution while utilizing tax advantages. This is discussed in greater detail in Chapter 18, The Return on Investment.

SOME CONSIDERATIONS ABOUT YOUR PRESENTATION TEAM

- Never take an army. One problem that can occur with a large group is too many people trying to respond to client questions at the same time. The resulting confusion can make you and your team seem disorganized and the presentation may come across like a scene from a bad movie.

- Do not invite more representatives from your company than will be in attendance from your prospect's company. If you do, they will feel as though your organization is overwhelming them.

- Always be positive.

- Continually qualify time frames for your specific decision

- Keep the sales process moving forward.

- Never ever intimidate, become pushy, or be overly aggressive, especially with a high level officer such as a Vice President. This behavior by the salesperson will do more damage than good.

- Leave your rubber sledgehammer in the trunk of your car!

- Educate by asking probing, qualifying questions.

Your presentation should address all of the company's objections. Thoroughly discuss your capabilities by presenting your FAB: Features that are translated into Advantages and finally Benefits.

An example of this very effective sales technique is as follows:
"Mr. Hopkins, you said you wanted greater response throughout the worldwide operation of ABC Corp. I'd like to present the latest technology that will help you achieve your goal."

Feature: *"First, I'd like to discuss our technology feature called 'remote storage'. This feature allows your organization to store information separately from the host computer."*

Advantage: *"And Mr. Hopkins, the major advantage to your organization is that anyone authorized by you can access this information from anywhere in the world."*

Benefit: *"The real benefit of remote storage, Mr. Hopkins, is that you can use it on any of your configured networks without taking up space on every separate server location throughout the world."*

Then try to probe your client to determine if this component is important in their decision-making process.
"Don't you think the greater efficiency and reduced cost of remote storage at a central location might be helpful to your organization?"

By asking this question, you are engaging your audience in your presentation. You are gauging their interest in various elements of your product and service offerings. You may be able to determine from your prospect's gathered representatives who is truly interested, who is not; who the real decision-makers are, who merely make recommendations. This meeting may further demonstrate the type of 'corporate culture' that exists within this company. The terminology of corporate culture reflects the attitudes, processes, and manner of conducting business related to this account. Every company exists and operates in a unique working environment. By understanding their culture, you can determine how to successfully sell your solution.

Try to stay on schedule. Your client's time must be utilized very effectively, especially when involving their high level executives. Maintain the schedule you devised with your itinerary or initial meeting agenda. That can be altered, of course, if these key executives ask pertinent questions which lead to meaningful discussion involving your solution. In that particular case, extending the time of this meeting is very positive to your sales efforts. But the allotment and use of extended time is their call.

It is usually normal for the sales professional to keep his sales team on track so that their discussions are not too long-winded. You are the traffic cop, smoothly intervening when necessary, and always in a courteous manner.

When the presentation has reached a natural conclusion, it is your responsibility to summarize your company's key capabilities, setting traps for your direct competitors.

This may be accomplished in the following manner:
"Mr. Hopkins, our remote storage capability is exactly the feature you want to automate your company. I know you're reviewing the Remington Diagnostic System, who is our direct competitor. I just want to point out the important difference between our system and theirs: Our system can be accessed remotely anywhere in the world from a remote location, including all of Europe, with extremely fast response time. The Remington System isn't accessible in Germany where you have a large operation."

This type of presentation does not slam your competition. You have merely presented a very key selling point in a concise and factual manner. That it's never a good idea to sell against a competitor in an emotional, destructive way bears repeating. Doing so will create a very unprofessional image of you in the client's mind. And that's not the image you want people to recall when they think about you.

Make sure that you showcase your organization in the most effective and positive manner. You and your team should:

- Offer true value to the customer.

- Listen carefully to the requirements and total vision of your audience.

- Never push your products, rather offer true definable business solutions.

- Offer capabilities after the needs, pains, and requirements of the client have been developed and/ or identified.

- Focus on the requirements of your audience, not on a memorized script or slide presentation.

- Once again, do not resort to high-pressure, strong-armed closing techniques.

- Analyze and discuss all questions and concerns of your client. Avoiding objections is not a professional option in a high level meeting.

- View the potential sale as a business partnership that culminates in a mutually beneficial transaction determined by straightforward conversation.

- Ask one last time if there is any further information you will need to know to make the best possible proposal.

- Determine with the client a mutually agreeable date for your next step.

In an overall sense, your prospect must be able to envision your solution and value proposition. They must feel your organization is a worthy business partner and be able to differentiate you from your competitors. They should feel you have a valid concern for their stability and growth. Finally, they should feel there is an open and honest communication path between the two of you.

On your part, one of the hardest steps in the sales process is about to take place: determining what was said, what was meant, and what are the key elements of your proposal.

GO WITH UPPER MANAGEMENT, DON'T GO IT ALONE

Having upper management involved with your sales presentation can provide the buy-in necessary for you to invest your time and manpower in an attempt to sell this account. I urge you to involve your management in this manner as often as possible. Should your opportunity prove bogus, operating without support could cause you irreparable damage.

chapter thirteen

Surveying Customer Requirements and the Art of Listening

Your team has just finished its sales presentation. In some cases, you've even sat through lunch with the prospective client during an on-site meeting. Now comes the most important part of the team process: determining what was actually said and deciding what it means. With as many as three different individuals participating from your sales team, it is interesting to discover how different each person's impressions of the same event can be.

Hopefully, everyone listened intently to your prospect's discussions. But, having been involved with hundreds of these meetings, I can tell you this is not always the case. First, the salesperson can become so 'hyped up' that much of what the customer said fell on deaf ears. Sometimes, the rep may desperately need to close some business quickly and is using wishful thinking to see this account as a prospect when in reality it isn't a closeable prospect.

Your technical or industry specialist may have had too little time to go into detail about why your various solutions may or may not be a good fit for the client. Because he is likely to be highly focused on technical data, he may not have captured the group dynamics that took place during his presentation.

Your Vice President may have had his mind on retrieving the information on his laptop that he has just presented. Further, he might be checking his watch to make sure he will not miss the plane for his next presentation. Moreover, your Vice President may have participated in so many similar presentations that they all have blended together and he may not even recall what was actually said in this one.

It's important for your team to meet as a group and discuss the presentation as soon after its completion as possible. Each of you should think beyond your specialty and personal concerns and collectively conclude what it will take to close this account. Constructive criticism is necessary as well so that each of you can determine what was accomplished and what was not.

Review this opportunity and discuss these questions:
- Were they interested?
- Did you have difficulty in getting their interest?
- Were they willing or unable to share their thoughts and concerns?
- Did they provide verbal and non-verbal cues acknowledging their approval?
- Were they satisfied that your presentation addressed all of their concerns?
- Did the decision-makers have a hidden agenda or will they allow your team a legitimate chance to close the deal?
- Was this just an exercise for the client to get a low price from you, which they can take back to their current vendor to get a reduced payment from them?
- Was your solution viewed as too complex and/or expensive?
- Is your prospect's team not expert or experienced in buying your product?
- Are a lot of your competitors bidding on this same opportunity?
- Will your solution require a drastic change in how your prospect currently does business?
- Were the members of the account's team obviously not on the same page?

Once the account has been qualified as a prospect, a list needs to be made of what you and your team have to do to close the sale. If your deliverables include things like training staff, free delivery and set up, or other company requirements, make sure your company can handle these commitments. Never provide so many perks that the final sale results in bad business — a situation where you don't make the money from the sale that you should.

Next, your sales team — with your guidance — needs to list the reasons why this opportunity is winnable:

- What is the customer application?
- Is there a logical reason or a compelling event that assures you this project is will happen?
- Is your solution competitive?
- Does it fit their business criteria?
- Is your relationship conducive to a mutually satisfying partnership?
- Can your team offer positive business value?
- Do you have support from your "coach" (inside salesperson) within the account?
- Has your team gained acceptance at the executive level?
- Is there a mesh within their organizational culture and your organization's philosophical code of operations?
- Is there true synergy between your respective organizations?

As a sales professional, you can never qualify too many times. It is essential to revisit the previous qualifying questions, especially after an important meeting, and always close the prospect for the next appropriate steps.

Here are three things you should always keep in mind throughout the entire sales process.

1. Who are your major competitors and what are they offering?
2. What are your goals and objectives unique to winning this opportunity?
3. What are the main challenges that must be overcome to win the sale?

After you have answered those questions, list your product and service offerings that will win the business.

The following components summary may assist you in determining sales opportunity:

- List the application or project summary.
- Review the business issues.
- What is the compelling event or criteria for moving forward?
- List the decision-making processes and their timeframes.
- What are your proposal solutions?
- Do you offer a distinct business value proposition?
- Define your sales strategy and objectives.
- Determine your action plan and timeline necessary for completion.
- Identify with whom your team should meet and determine why. Don't forget to review their financial standing:
- Is your prospect financially sound and growing?
- Do they have current and/or long term funding in place?
- Does this sale offer both long and short-term high margin dollar revenue?
- Is there any risk in moving forward with this opportunity?
- Could the prospect be a solid referenceable account?

Planning is the key to creating a winning proposal solution, one that will set your team apart from your competitors. Success will not happen without careful listening and evaluation by your team together. Remember, the art of listening can be even more important to the successful sales professional than speaking.

To be successful at Selling in the Real World, you must know what will it take not only to compete, but ultimately to win!

chapter fourteen

Understanding the Organizational Chart of your Client

It is often a total waste of your time to make presentations to those who are not the ultimate decision-makers. Frontline or middle managers may only make a recommendation about whether or not their superior should listen to you make your presentation again. If you can present initially to the person who decides, the process for all involved will be quicker and smoother. So, the big question is: "Who are these men and women?"

LET'S START AT THE TOP AT THE C LEVEL.

The Chief Executive Officer [CEO], runs the company. He or she is responsible for everyone and reports directly to the Board of Directors/Trustees. The CEO is extremely difficult to get an audience with. But if your solution is costly, believe me the CEO will review it. CEOs focus on results. Make sure your solution details how your product will make the CEO's company more efficient. The CEO will want to know if your product offers a unique solution that allows predictable forecasting, will be financially rewarding for their company, and will show a profit as a direct result of your solution.

The Chief Financial Officer [CFO] will review how to lower the cost of operations. He or she may get monetary or stock bonuses if the organization increases profitability by decreasing expenses. Sometimes that equates to cutting jobs or downsizing. Along with the Vice President of Finance, the CFO will usually attempt to reduce the cost of customer service. They look to lower the amount of money tied into the company's inventory. Other areas of concern include fine tuning overhead by reducing expenditures. As such, the head of finance always looks at the bottom line, not at increasing productivity by spending more money.

The Chief Information Officer[CIO] is responsible for the company's technology systems and their productivity. Does the organization possess the wherewithal to favorably compete in a highly technical world? Has the company approved the budget to upgrade the computers, the security systems, the communication systems, etc.? And have these costs been justified enough to pass the scrutiny of the financial people in the corporation? Information technology individuals usually report to the CIO.

The Chief Operating Officer [COO] wants efficiency in the organization. This individual usually takes the middle ground between spending money and increasing efficiency. Thus, this person is not as cost conscious as the members of the financial department but is also not as driven to upgrade technology as are his counterparts in the information department.

The President reports to the CEO, as do most other C Level people. The President is responsible to increase stock value and share price. This person is targeted with increasing profits in the company. Usually, he is the public spokesperson for the organization.

Under this high-level executive resides a wide range of managerial levels consisting of various Vice Presidents. On occasion, larger organizations may include Senior Vice Presidents who may have been awarded this advanced title in recognition of many years of service to the company. This individual may even have other Vice Presidents reporting to him/her. A Senior Vice President is usually in line to become the next C-level employee. This person can be a Vice President from any of the following disciplines.

The Vice-President of Marketing is tagged with reviewing and implementing top quality leading-edge products and services. This individual wants to track business analyses that emphasize the predictability of their company's products versus those of their direct competitors.

The Vice-President of Sales strives for consistency in achieving all sales goals to enable the majority of the sales people to meet or overachieve their quotas. This individual must be accurate in his sales forecasting. It is also his responsibility to ensure that sales strategies and training are in place for the organization's revenue growth.

The Vice-President of Manufacturing is charged with providing a top quality product at the best possible cost. This person must meet production schedules with desirable customer delivery dates. Individuals like the Director of Quality Control and the Plant Manager usually report to this Vice President.

The Vice-President of Customer Service gauges the corporation's customer expectations. This individual desires to increase the responsiveness to the company's valued customer base. Existing business can be the easiest resource from which to increase overall revenue. Thus, maintaining and supporting the customer base is the prime way to increase revenues and prevent losing customers to a competitor.

Other key executives may be found in some companies; however, these are generally the most common.

Knowing what each C Level executive is responsible for will allow successful sales personnel to effectively target the correct decision-maker within an organization and to create the appropriate Elevator Pitch (complete with Return on Investment) that will effectively sell the specific requirements to those key individuals.

DOMINANT PERSON	FINANCIAL PERSON
EMOTIONAL RECOMMENDER	CONTEMPLATIVE EVALUATOR

NOTES

chapter fifteen

Decision-makers and their Personality Traits

While it is absolutely true that everyone is different and that no two people are exactly the same, it is also true all of us have similarities. When similarities are established, patterns can be predicted. This has been my experience when selling to executive management..

For example, a particular Senior Vice President may exhibit a strong Type A style personality, one that is usually very opinionated and does not take too kindly to disagreement. The salesperson who succeeds with the Type A personality usually allows that person to freely express his views and restates them back to him.

> **Type A:** *"I have been here more than ten years, young man. I've seen hot shot employees come and I've seen them go. I never try to guess at anything. I always want all the facts before I make a decision. I don't listen to noise coming out of left field. Understand?"*

> **Salesperson:** *"Of course, sir. I believe I fully understand your concerns. You want accurate data compiled from factual information. Statements made without factual information are an absolute waste of your time."*

> **Type A:** *"Absolutely."*

FOUR TYPES OF PERSONALITIES

The Dominant Person often has a Type A personality. He requires effective listening and indirect probing statements by the salesperson. He should not be challenged. Don't mistake the Dominant Person's abrupt manner as being offensive. Simply stated, he is telling you exactly what you need to know in order to make a sale to his organization. Because of this propensity for direct and straightforward conversation, the Dominant Person can be the least difficult executive to sell. For the most part, this individual reveals his mind and has no hidden agendas. He clearly expresses what it will take to satisfy his requirements. There is no guesswork. Although the Dominant Person requires information to make decisions, often those decisions will strongly be influenced by what seem like gut reactions. Gut reactions are not the intuitive behavior we think they are but rather the result of extremely quick and complex reasoning decisions made by a mind working at the subconscious level such that the resultant response seems more like a feeling than a calculation.

The Dominant Person's outspokenness can be a valued leadership quality and he often rises quickly through the company due to this driving personality.

The Financial Person looks at the bottom line. He evaluates every business decision financially. This individual is also straightforward and does not operate on emotion. For the most part, the Financial Person will accumulate the total cost of your proposal, ask for appropriate discounts, review the return on investment in terms of added capabilities plus tax advantages, and then evaluate whether your offering is favorable for his business. He will evaluate current trends and market climates and decide if his company can afford the money to maintain or increase market share at this time. The Financial Person is usually even-tempered, sometimes considered the nice person. They hold high level positions because they compile wide-ranging factual knowledge and downplay their subjective qualities.

The sales approach to the Financial Person, should be straightforward. Provide this individual all the facts – the good as well as some that are negative, as long as those negative characteristics will not be "showstoppers."

Sales Executive: *"Mr. O'Connor, I want to make you aware that our company values quality and to ensure your product meets our aggressive standards, we normally quote a two week turn-around, even though our competitors only quote one week."*

Financial Person: *"I'm not happy with this delivery date, but I'm glad you explained this to me now. I admire your honesty."*

While your honesty and integrity are being honored here — and those are characteristics that will enhance your opportunity to successfully sell your product or service — it is never a good idea to present a major disadvantage during your presentation. If the objection is large enough, such as a significant price difference or a major operating deficiency, your potential sale could be blown right out of the water. The best course of action is to present the positives and allow the decision-maker to do his due diligence and uncover what he considers to be the objections to your product. Hopefully, those objections will not be so significant that you cannot overcome them when they are presented and prevent you from completing the sale.

The Emotional Recommender has a very strong emotional base, which is often very subjective. This individual may have been trained on a specific methodology or technology and cannot conceive of any other possible means to accomplish the task. Emotional Recommenders are very difficult individuals to win over, especially if they have a strong connection with your competitor. Unfortunately, these individuals are often the first level decision-makers. Meeting the Emotional Recommender before making contact with his direct supervisor is one of the more difficult paths to successful sale.

In the technology field, a Network Manager who reports to the Director of Information Technology illustrates this scenario. The Network Manager may have been thoroughly trained and even have had engineering experience with IBM, for example. As such, a Cisco sales executive may, in most likelihood, have difficulty in attempting to interest this Network Manager in Cisco technology management systems. Perhaps his best opportunity would be to discuss the advantages of his product with the Network Manager's direct supervisor, the Director of Information Technology. This scenario will still be a tough sell since few organizations have enough difficulties to completely change from a current vendor. But without making that contact with the Director of Information Technology, the sales executive will not know that for sure. Never assume anything in your career as a salesperson. You may, in fact, find the right person who wants to incorporate a technological upgrade by either completely changing their vendor's entire system or even part of it. Part of something is always a better alternative than zero percent of nothing!

The Contemplative Evaluator usually does the initial research on your company's products and services. He or she can be very difficult to sell because this person is not a decision-maker. He or she is simply collecting information and presenting the findings to his or her direct manager. The Contemplative Evaluator constantly requests information. This individual is always analyzing in an attempt to understand how everything operates. The Contemplative Evaluator may even contact the sales representative several times to collect additional information even after a decision has been made! This individual is very difficult to pin down! The Contemplative Evaluator will attempt to shield the sales executive from the key decision-maker. In this way, this individual is similar to a sales screen, although he or she can be a deal breaker. Never take the Contemplative Evaluator lightly, but never depend on this person to make a decision involving your product or service.

Both the Emotional Recommender and Contemplative Evaluator are entry-level management types. While neither makes final decisions, neither should be ignored for they can stop your sales effort dead in its tracks. They will usually not sell your product or service for you. It is uncertain whether or not they will pass along positive recommendations about the purchase of your product. Recommenders and Evaluators generally report to a Vice President or a front line manager similar to the Network Manager.

So that you don't get boxed out by lower level management, do your best to secure appointments with decision-makers first. Should this not be possible, try to start with the highest level manager available to you.

chapter sixteen

Creating Value for Large Sales Opportunities

Sales with price tags of six or more figures often require another level of information-gathering meetings. These meetings are usually part of the buying culture of the prospective client and as such may vary widely in approach and specific details. The intent of these meetings is for both sides to become totally clear on the objectives, needs, and deliverables connected to the impending sale. Not all sales processes will include this additional C-Level interview. In some cases, the time spent on these exchanges of information can even become billable.

The written document resulting from these meetings is sometimes called an assessment — or study — and is provided to the client. Assessments are not designed to be a final proposal, but rather a gathering of all necessary information needed to be in complete compliance with the requirements of the potential client's buying process. Assessment documents also may be billable or non-billable.

Key how to points most clients will want to cover may include:
- Increasing productivity and efficiency
- Producing higher overall revenue
- Reducing expenses
- Lowering structural costs
- Attracting new clientele
- Retaining and expanding the customer base
- Increasing market share

- Expanding profitability
- Increasing stock dividend
- Increasing positive awareness for the stockholders.

In short, your organization must establish value to this potential client. Value is not what your product/service provides but rather the result from the product/service you sell them. Not what the product/service does, but what the product/service will allow the company to do as a result of purchasing it. Fulfilling the Value Objective may be the most important step in the entire sales process. Getting the customer to recognize and appreciate the value you bring is the professional sales executive's responsibility.

This approach of gathering valuable information from their executive staff provides you with exposure to their attitudes, goals, agendas, and observations.

This exposure can provide you with a definite advantage over your competition while allowing you the opportunity to:
- Stress your company's strengths
- Understand your competitor's strengths and weaknesses
- Set traps for your competition
- Gain executive input into your solution.

As a result of this style of information gathering, your final solution is, in essence, devised by their executive staff.

Even if this survey is costly in terms of your staff time and is not billable, this exposure to C-Level executive management is the most successful way to secure a favorable decision from your client.

I can't stress this enough: Don't get caught up performing large amounts of non-billable work or research for lower levels of management. This is a great way to waste your valuable time and resources. When you sell to the wrong audience, your efforts most often will be lost. Don't cut your career as an executive sales professional short by not selling at the C-Level. Have the drive to secure high level appointments and provide the value they expect.

Make sure the information gathered at this C-Level interaction is included in your final proposal.

It should be used to:
- Give the client deliverable solutions
- Satisfy their requirements for product/service
- Make them feel they contributed to your solution
- Make your solution difficult to turn down.

Remember that final proposals should contain alternative solutions so that when more than one key executive reviews it there will be more than one opinion as to what's the most important reason to purchase, or not purchase, your product/service. Proposals should have options that address as many different issues as is feasible and practical. In that way, their executives will find themselves arguing about which of your proposed solutions is the best choice instead of arguing about whether your one-solution proposal should be chosen or not chosen. These alternative options could be, for example, a full-blown-package with all the bells and whistles, a standard package, or an economy package. In that way, they can choose between low cost, high capability, and something in between.

Understanding each executive's priorities will help you sell accordingly. This pre-qualified close could be appropriate to uncover their level of interest in your solutions:

"All right, Mr. O'Connor. If I provide this solution at the price we have stated in the form of a proposal, would you agree to move forward and authorize our solution?"

After any question like this, try to surface new objections. These objections must be discovered prior to the completion of your final proposal and the sooner you deal with them, the sooner they can be solved and overcome.

You will be able to satisfy executive decision-makers if you help them keep in mind that:
- Your proposal will have a positive impact on their customer service.
- Your goods or services will streamline their operation regardless of company politics, divisions, and/or multiple locations throughout the world.

- Your solution will enable them to surpass their competition regardless of any current or future economic trend.
- Your organization will increase their revenues and stock value. This strong selling point can be presented to the Board of Trustees, effectively enhancing the position of all executive staff involved in your solution.

While this C-Level meeting may not be a requirement for all sales processes, especially lower-cost sales, the elements contained should all be addressed at all level of sales at all times. Keep in mind that you may not have the opportunity or requirement for the more formal approach this chapter describes.

chapter seventeen

Offering Client Solutions
Creating the Proposal

The sales proposal is your finished product. It is the end result of all your meetings, your survey of customer requirements, and your research of company information and materials. It is the compilation of the seemingly endless work both you and your company have completed to date. It is your sales team's earnest attempt to solve a business problem for your potential client. Once delivered to and signed by the customer, a proposal becomes a legally binding document with which your company will have to live.

On many occasions, the proposal is delivered along with the final contract for their legal department to review. It should go without saying that this document must accurately reflect the views of your organization. It is not advisable to complete your proposal without having it reviewed by the appropriate members of your organization.

To deliver a proposal that does not incorporate management approval might be the most rapid way to be terminated from your sales position. Never assume that the final draft of your proposal will be acceptable to your company. As in any facet of sales, it is never good practice to assume — especially when it comes to a legally binding document!

With that in mind, let's review what should be contained in your final proposal.

Your proposal should begin with a hard-hitting, to-the-point letter addressed to the main decision-maker. The following document is an example of such a letter.

· ———————— · ———————— ·

Larry Sternlieb Seminars, LLC (LSS) would like to thank you for the opportunity to submit this sales training proposal.

Spending time, energy, and financial resources on improving your sales team is one of the most beneficial investments a company can make. Making that investment with Larry Sternlieb Seminars is your most effective choice.

LSS is a proven entity in assisting organizations through productive sales training. We provide your sales staff with practical, real-world habits and practices which generate positive results that send more money to your bottom line.

I am certain you will find the Larry Sternlieb Seminars LLC approach to sales training to be innovative, unique, and highly effective.

If you have any further questions after reviewing this document, feel free to contact me. We look forward to our next steps.

Respectfully,
Larry Sternlieb

· ———————— · ———————— ·

This letter will set the stage for your completed document. After a Title Page and a Table of Contents Page, include the following segments:

An executive summary A discussion of the main components of your presentation. Included in that summary should be a solutions/benefits section, highlighting your areas of strength and industry leadership. Some of your Executive Summary might include:

- Product benefits statements
- Commitment to customer satisfaction
- Description of staff and service
- Flexibility to meet changing requirements
- Solution benefits:
    1. Integration of your product/services
    2. Flexibility of your product/service
    3. Increased productivity
    4. Increased end-user satisfaction.

The company overview follows the executive summary and contains the following items:

- Mission Statement
- Your vision and business philosophy
- Core values
- Management philosophy
- Your product and/or service overview
- Company history
- Your locations and/or organizational structure.

The products/services overview follows the company overview and should include:

- Product hardware overview
- Parts management
- Service and support system
- Tracking system
- Customer call escalation management
- Customer satisfaction
- Your company's knowledge base of products.

The professional services overview would be next for proposals in the financial and technical consulting fields and may include:

- Consulting practices breakdown
- IT planning and consulting services
- Project/program management
- Enterprise systems
- Enterprise management
- Engineering service
- Financial assessment and planning
- Return on investment disclosure
- Return on equity overview
- Asset management

The pricing module displays various pricing options. Keep in mind there may be more than one solution recommended and those various options must be presented on an individual basis, specific to the needs of each company. If you are selling a product, then it would be advisable to offer leasing options as well. Obviously, there may be accrued trade in values of your customer's existing equipment, which should also be presented. Maintenance costs, when necessary, should be included.

A disclaimer page, depending upon the type of proposal you have prepared.

If your proposal is the result of an RFP (Request For Proposal), the following additional areas may be necessary to include in your proposal:

Proprietary notice contains confidential information of Larry Sternlieb Seminars, LLC (LSS). In consideration of the receipt of this document, ABC Corporation agrees not to reproduce or make this information available in any manner to non-ABC Corporation employees and persons outside the group directly responsible for evaluation of its contents.

Assumptions This is been prepared in accordance with ABC Corporation's requirements as of today's date based upon information provided to LSS and represents LSS's best judgments based upon such information.

Options Certain services and programs contained in this proposal and overview of capabilities may not be included in the prices quoted. These references are included for information purposes only pending subsequent discussions to clarify the ABC Corporation need and LSS's proposed offering, including pricing.

Award If LSS is selected to supply some or all the services described in this Proposal to ABC Corporation, LSS will work with ABC Corporation to mutually agree to a suitable purchase agreement and a comprehensive implementation plan fully acceptable to both LSS and ABC Corporation. Duly authorized representatives of both parties will sign the agreement before services are rendered. The purchase agreement should include such elements as: scope of work descriptions, specifications and appropriate terms and conditions of sale.

In the event this proposal is required by ABC Corporation to be incorporated into a purchase agreement as an exhibit and in the event any portion of such proposal conflicts with the terms and conditions of the underlying purchase agreement, the terms of the underlying agreement shall take precedence.

This proposal document must be personally presented to high-level management, including C Level executives, Board members, Presidents, and Owners of the organization or other relevant company individuals.

Remember: Never present your proposal to a midrange manager, like a Purchasing Manager, Telecommunications or Information Technology Manager, or company consultant. Decision-makers are almost always C-Level executives. Middle managers follow trends dictated by executive management. Their livelihood depends on being security-minded. That is, they focus first on keeping their jobs. They do not like taking risks or making significant decisions. Their goal is simply to collect and accumulate as much information as possible, for knowledge is power in job security and retention.

The C-Level and/or executive staff always makes the important decisions involving products and services. That is the audience you want when presenting your final proposal. Try to include your inside salesperson or 'coach' to assist your sales efforts. This inside person can also serve as a straightforward sounding board to gauge your level of acceptance.

During the creation of your proposal, keep these concepts in mind:

1. Maintain good business rapport
2. Constantly ask for opinions about and seek attitudes regarding your company and its solution.
3. Be honest. Never lie about your capabilities.
4. Distinguish why your solution will create value and benefit to their company.
5. Remember that salespeople are many times not trusted. However, partners are not only trusted, but valued.

By this process, the customer will both objectively and subjectively view you and your organization as a partner.

THREE COPIES MAKE GOOD SENSE

It is good practice to have a minimum of three original copies of all pertinent contracts printed when closing your sales orders. Why? Many companies require more than one original copy from their sales person, some buyers require two copies, and it's always a good idea to have an extra copy with you just in case.

chapter eighteen

The Return on Investment

Regardless of, and in addition to, their specific needs, purchasers of products and services are all looking for one thing — justification for their purchase. The person responsible for suggesting and/or approving the purchase must be able to prove to anyone and everyone that this purchase was the right thing to do, that this purchase improved the company, and most of all, that this purchase was a good Return on Investment (ROI).

ROI simply means the ratio of the dollar value of the results (return) compared to the dollar value of the initial expenditure (investment). The better that percentage, the better the purchase; at least from a financial point of view.

As a successful salesperson, you will need to prove to your potential customer that the ROI of your product/ service is good; that buying what you are selling is a smart financial decision.

Good ROI has always been of paramount concern for successful companies. Your ability to prove a good ROI will directly impact your ability to sell your product/service to your potential customer.

To be successful, you will need to know:
- The needs of the decision-maker.
- How they cost-justify your product/service.

- What specifically will your customer look at to determine ROI?
- How will they measure their ROI?
- If they are using a software portal or another measurement tool to determine ROI, can you have a list of the data required to produce their evaluation?
- How much are they willing to spend?
- Can you stay within their budget?

To begin determining ROI, you will need to know if your potential customer uses your product or service as an Operation Expense or as a Capital Investment. For example, if your product is computer paper, this may be an operating expense and thus deductible as a taxable expense of up to 100%. If your product is computer equipment, the expense may be a write-off and you may be required to show a depreciation schedule over a three to five year period.

If the transaction is a lease, then you can accept trade-in value for your customer's existing equipment, which can become a down payment on your equipment. Then you can develop a depreciation schedule to write off the allowable portion of the remaining cost of your customer's expenditure .

Another positive ROI strategy is to show how the equipment maintenance, if applicable, will be a lesser monthly cost in comparison to your customer maintaining their older equipment. Providing a year of free maintenance including a warranty period will also improve ROI.

The purchase of new equipment from you may eliminate entry-level employees from your client's payroll. Additionally, the advanced features of your equipment may eliminate time spent on certain projects.

Finally, consider and include all tax advantages and financial credits. The net cost to the potential client of purchasing your product/service could be significantly less than he or she expected. This low overall or monthly expense could be the single benefit that swings the deal.

Benefits to the potential client such as these will increase the ROI and can be used to justify the expenditure on your product or service. The successful salesperson will understand the importance of good ROI and will be able to use it as a tool to complete the sale.

The return on investment credits can be either soft or hard dollars. Hard dollars refers to the amount of money your customer will receive for equipment trade-in, discounts, or tax credits. Soft dollars are those that involve assumed cost returns like greater efficiency or the reduction of entry level jobs due to the implementation of your product or service. Both hard and soft credits should be utilized to cost justify your prospect's expenditure.

Once you have prepared the ROI analysis to be included with your proposal, the customer must then engage in due diligence to determine if they will authorize the approval to purchase your product/service.

Their executive staff will be looking at:

- The deliverable product and/or service versus the cost.
- The soft and hard credits versus the actual cost.
- Their budget to decide if money has been allocated or is available.
- Unanimous buy-in from C-Level executives.

Keep in mind it only takes one C-Level executive to effectively kill any deal. To prevent a scenario like that, your ROI should include the cost in hard and soft dollars to the potential client should they not accept your proposal.

The following are the most common concerns of C-Level executives with regard to sales proposals presented for consideration. Your ability to anticipate these concerns and address them will go a long way in determining the outcome of your proposal. By addressing and solving these problems, the hard cost to a qualified prospect assumes diminished importance.

President: Are our company's stock shares increasing in value? Are profits high?

Vice President of Sales: Are our sales representatives obtaining their sales goals? Are we delivering products on time to the customer's satisfaction? Is our forecasting accurate?

Vice President of Marketing: Does the data from the sales department show our customers are satisfied? Has our company maintained and/or increased market share over their competitors?

Distribution Manager: Are our deliveries to customers on time? Are distribution costs rising higher than the cost of sales? Is inventory accurate? Is turnaround timely?

Vice President of Manufacturing: Are our delivery dates unacceptable? Is our cost of producing quality goods or services too great? Is our company manufacturing products within a reasonable timeline?

Plant Manager: Is our organization producing quality products and/or services? Is our delivery schedule consistent or does it change frequently? Are our customers returning many items?

Providing solutions to their problems will make the buyer even more certain that doing business with your company is not only their best choice, but also their only choice.

Although I do not believe a quality sales professional needs to be a Certified Public Accountant (CPA), it is necessary to have a handle on some financial aspects of your client and be able to discuss them competently. This is especially important when interfacing with the President or any C-Level executive.

You can review your potential client's earnings and investments at various websites, such as Hoovers.com, Yahoo News, or Quicken.com.

Once there, you will also be able to look for and discover this type of information:

- Dividend Information: Yield, Payout Ratio
- Profit Margins: Pre-Tax, Operating Margin and Net
- Per Share Data: Earnings, Book Value, Cash Flow
- Financial Conditions: Quick Ratio, Current Ratio, Long Term Debt/Equity
- Price Ratio: Return on Equity
- Growth Rates: Sales, EPS, Dividend
- Revenue History: Millions of US Dollars for Past Two Years
- Earnings per Share: US Dollars for Past Two Years
- Short Interest
- Stock Price Historical Return

The better you understand and are able to intelligently discuss these issues, the more respect your client will have for you and consequently your solutions as outlined in your proposal. The process of obtaining this information will greatly enhance your understanding of the client's operation and allow you to better target your solution to their needs.

A note of caution: if you find you truly do not understand these terms, it is better to avoid using them than to use them incorrectly in a manner that might seem like an uneducated bluff.

The greater your financial insight into your potential client's business operations, the greater your ability to accurately and effectively communicate the Return on Investment your product or service will provide, thus greatly improving your ability to win their trust and get the sale.

CONNECTING WITH YOUR CLIENT

Really top-notch professional sales representatives take the time to understand what's happening in the world around them and their clients; and they use that knowledge to show their understanding of how events are affecting the proposed client, both positively and negatively. They also are careful in the use of that knowledge to avoid creating boundaries and fences along non-business-related topics such as politics, religion, etc.

You are not trying to create an us-versus-them situation but rather to show that you understand how life can affect them, their decision to move forward, and their bottom line.

And that you are providing a solution to help them deal with the world around them.

NOTES

chapter nineteen

Closing Out the Competition

Americans cherish their opportunity to realize their dreams, both personal and financial, and become the person they choose to become. That opportunity exists as a direct result of our freedom to compete. Because our society has been free to compete, every strong, viable organization has, or will soon have, a strong, capable competitor. If an idea is good for one, it is just as good, if not better, for another. Often, the second company in the marketplace becomes the industry leader. That happens because the second company had to fight hard to become better than the first company. Good competition builds strong business. As no coin has only one side, selling automatically seems to come with competition. The question in sales becomes: how do you contend with your competitors?

First of all, don't fear competition. Not only do competitors make you smarter, stronger, and better, but your competitors provide the measuring tool that your prospect uses to gauge your proposed solution. Being successful in your quest to sell to your potential client is actually easier when you have a competitor against which to compare your products and services. When there are competitors, potential clients better understand your product or service. All they need to do is compare the points you present them. When your company is the only one in the field, not only do you have to convince the potential client to buy from you, but you have to educate that client as to the necessity of your product and service in the first place. They will be surprised, if not skeptical, that no competition exists.

The concept of closing out your competition has been referred to several times before. This chapter will deal with some specific, targeted ways to achieve that goal.

For ease of understanding this concept, let's imagine a romantic scenario in which you are trying to win the heart of a significant other. Not only are you trying to convince that person that they should choose you, you are trying to position yourself as being a superior choice to any other choices in suitors they may have, whether real or simply potential at the moment. If you ignore a competing suitor, they will not simply disappear. Rather they will be busy pitching themselves as the best solution. If you overreact to a competing suitor and verbally attack them, demeaning their character and actions, you may engender backlash against you and in support of them. Your significant other may actually be forced into defending her choice of someone else.

In sales, the same is true. Your competitor must be seriously considered as a strong and powerful opponent who, at one level or another, has been allowed to compete for your client's business. You cannot degrade this individual or group without the risk of forcing your client into a defensive posture, which, under severe pressure, might just result in a sympathy sale to your competitor. Attacking a competitor is always an unprofessional approach that will almost always create a negative image of you in the client's eye.

Consequently, your competitors should be openly and even-handedly discussed with your potential client in a matter-of-fact manner as shown in Chapter 6, 'Qualifying the Suspect.'

What you want to learn about your competitor is what does your prospect like about his solution? What does he dislike? As you learn these, you are collecting information to build a case against your competitor in a manner similar to a lawyer preparing for litigation.

Remember that the process of collecting information and then later comparing and contrasting your deliverable solution versus that of your competitor must be presented in a calm, but confident manner.

A conversation of this type may proceed as follows:

> **Salesperson:** *"Mr. O'Connor, I know you like some of the features of Marty Simon's sales training program. I believe you are very wise to be evaluating more than one option before deciding upon a selected vendor. If you allow me, I would like to discuss the inherent differences between Mr. Simon's product and LSS. Would that be possible at this time?"*

Once you gain their acceptance, bring up the areas your client likes and dislikes from the solution offered by your competitor. Engage your prospect in a nonthreatening conversation. To win their business, you must uncover your client's attitudes regarding your competition. It's to the advantage of your potential client to reveal your competitor's information so that you can effectively compete. The more each of you knows about the other, the better for the potential client. Most importantly, your prospect can effectively compare and contrast your fit with his company. If your client does not share competitive information with you, he may be using you simply as leverage to receive a better price from your competitor.

Once you know what your prospect likes and dislikes about the competition, set "traps" by raising important points that in all likelihood will be discussed between your prospect and your competitors. Simply put, a trap is a statement — or series of statements — that brings attention to the weakness of your competition. Make sure your traps are definite, inherent advantages that your solution has. By interactive discussions with your customer, explain your advantages in language they can understand. Always demonstrate why your features and advantages will benefit your customer.

> **Salesman:** *"Mr. O'Connor, did you know our organization guarantees customer support for every major city in the United States? Since you have sales offices in thirty major cities in America, then nationwide service coverage must be very important to your company."*

> **Mr. O'Connor:** *"Yes, that is extremely important. We cannot afford to have down time with our computer systems. Yes, we must have nationwide coverage."*

Salesman: *"Well, Mr. O'Connor, our organization has a national network of service coverage across the United States and Canada. We guarantee two-hour response time after receiving your phone call. I understand that you are also reviewing the Great Hope Company. Did you know that they are in only twelve cities?"*

Mr. O'Connor: *"Why no, we were not aware of that."*

Salesperson: *"Were you aware that they would not guarantee a temporary replacement for any of your computers, should they need servicing?"*

Mr. O'Connor: *"We certainly didn't know that. Well, this definitely will force us to review our evaluation process."*

If your prospect diminishes his opinion of your competitor and improves his impression of how your company can benefit him, then you can succeed in closing out your competitor.

At the same time, be realistic with your sales team:

- Determine if you have a high probability of being chosen over your competitor.
- Be honest in this evaluation process.
- Review the buying criteria: e.g. price, capability, service,
- Properly forecast the percentage of success you may have in closing this opportunity over your direct competitor.

chapter twenty

Overcoming Obstacles

Closing a sales opportunity involves more than just defeating your competition. As discussed throughout this book, there are many roadblocks — hidden and obvious — within and surrounding every potential sale. After spending quantities of time in the sales process it is foolish to overlook or ignore possible internal issues. Each account has several decision-makers who decide whether your solution is accepted or not. Each decision-maker has different agendas, both company-related and personal. Always expect the unexpected.

I said before that I've worked on huge opportunities that were fully qualified, that I felt certain would close, that, much to my chagrin, did not. For the most part they didn't close because I didn't complete this very necessary phase of the sales cycle. It's disheartening to make a successful presentation only to fail to get the sale because you were not able to overcome objections. There is never commission paid for almost selling a customer.

Customer objections fester deep in decision-makers' minds. They come from a wide range of sources, including your competitor as well as from inside your potential customer's company. Objections will remain unknown to the executive salesperson until they are brought out through repeated questioning and discussions.

It is a positive in the sales process when prospects state their objections. Once an objection is verbalized, it is no longer an objection but rather a concern — and concerns can be overcome. Unstated objections are a major cause for losing sales. However, the prospect's verbalized objections should be viewed as their way of expressing their actual desires and requirements.

Your prospect may state that your price is too high or that your service is not all encompassing, etc.

Simply restate that objection in the following manner:

> **Mr. O'Connor:** "I really like your service. But I do feel it is a bit too expensive."
>
> **Salesperson:** "Mr. O'Connor, if I understand you clearly, you are concerned about our price, feeling that it may be too expensive. Is that correct?"
>
> **Mr. O'Connor:** "Well yes, I do. I feel your price is higher than your competition."
>
> **Salesperson:** "I understand, Mr. O'Connor. If I were in your position, I too, would want to make sure I was getting my money's worth. Now let me explain the added value you're receiving for your additional investment."

The formula for overcoming objections

- Surface the prospect's objection
- Restate that objection back to the prospect
- Acknowledge the prospect has a valid concern
- Gain the prospect's agreement
- Explain why that concern is unfounded.

By this process, the salesperson has completely turned around the prospect's objection and replaced it as a mutual objective. The notion of transforming a seemingly definite no (an objection) into a definite yes (an objective) is the process of fully educating your prospect so that he can make a positive buying decision. As such, customer objections are really a request for more information.

As a top sales executive, it is your objective to surface all objections, which are really only concerns. The surfacing of objections allows the salesperson to continue the sales process and ultimately reach an agreement that both parties can live with. Objections should always be welcomed as another positive step toward the completion of the sale.

Make sure all customer objections are surfaced:

Salesperson: *"Mr. O'Connor now that we have discussed each of your concerns, are there any other areas about which you are uncertain?"*

Let him tell you those uncertainties. If you are a trusted partner, your prospect will reveal all his concerns. Remember, it takes only one uncertain concern or issue to stop the sales process. Don't allow that to happen.

Other circumstances that could jeopardize your sale include internal policies such as the creation of a purchase order from the purchasing department. To avoid this, ask what other formal processes or internal policies must be acknowledged to facilitate this sale. I have had experience with Purchasing Departments that delayed my large sale for months. The Purchasing Department must justify their existence and will, on occasion, make the sale difficult for a sales professional. Know that this can happen and be prepared to satisfy the requirements of that department.

The Board of Directors will want to review most large expenditures. It would be advisable to ask if you should accompany their executive staff to the board meeting to fully explain and answer any questions. You should always offer to assist your client's efforts, not try to upstage them. Cover all your bases as a valued business partner by fully supporting the efforts of your customer.

We've said that confidential or private circumstances, such as a competitor's father being on your client's Board of Directors or executive staff, are always potential obstacles.

If your competitor has an edge like this, you need to overcome that obstacle as early as possible. Once an obstacle such as this has been determined, the executive sales professional must convince all other decision-makers to choose his solution and try to neutralize any others who might favor your competitor.

Sometimes, it is not possible to convince everyone to buy from you. If your internal obstacle is the CEO or Chairman of the Board, then you might have an overwhelming real-world problem.

Lastly, discover if there are any outside influences that might sway the decision-makers. Outsiders with influence might be consultants. Consultants often have the confidence of your client and their opinions can be highly valued, completely throwing your sale into a tailspin. Consultants are usually subjective and politically connected to an executive within your account. If you have never been actively involved with consultants, trying to avoid them or not selling them in a manner similar to the rest of your account's executive staff can throw you for a loop!

Consultants must be sold to with the same intensity as any other decision-maker. This can actually work to your advantage by trying to become the consultant's business partner. Offer that individual the opportunity to work on accounts that you can introduce him into.

If the consultant specializes in a distinct SIC code/or business type such as higher education, then offer to establish an informal or even a formal marketing campaign to jointly sell that vertical market. That proposition can produce additional earnings for the consultant and position you as a business partner, instilling confidence in you and your proposed solutions.

As unlikely as it might seem, objections are a positive when it comes to sales. Without objections being verbalized, the sales professional will not have the opportunity to overcome them. Verbalized objections become a customer concern. Once satisfied, concerns become positive assets or sales objectives to assist in securing your sale.

Get your customers to talk. In this instance, silence is not golden!

chapter twenty-one

Is this Good Business?

The final hurdle to be faced before closing the sale comes from an unlikely source: the company that employs you! Review this potential account sale with your sales team. Solicit their input. Do your manager and his manager and, if necessary, your manager's manager and his boss like this opportunity? The executives of your company must believe that the potential sale of this client is good business or they may not approve all your hard work.

So, what exactly does "good business" mean?

Good business simply means that approving the sale will result in a positive outcome for your company.

Specifically, good business can be any or several of these things:

>**Large Volume.** The sale results in many units being sold at one time or repeatedly over a long period of time.

>**Repeat Sales.** The sale provides the opportunity for additional and/or consistent revenue streams.

>**High Profit Margins.** The sale generates a high return of dollars to your company after covering expenses.

Low Initial Margins with Promise. Although the initial sale may not produce much revenue, accomplishing the sale begins the process of promising, producing, or guaranteeing future sales at volume and/or higher margins. This would be a door-opener sale.

A Name Account. This is a well-known, well respected company, often a member of the Fortune 500 club. A sale to a name account can, at future strategic times, be referred by you and the rest of your sales staff to potential clients, enhancing the value of your product. Such an account could even become a showcase account, one that would allow you to bring potential clients to their facility so you can demonstrate your product/service in a working environment. In an ultimate scenario, this company's executives would participate in your future demonstrations adding their support and testimony to your product/ service.

Buy the Business. Sometimes to make the sale it might require your organization to drop its price so drastically and/or reduce revenue so significantly that you make little or no money in the process. Essentially, this means you are choosing to buy the business. Sales of this sort must be justified to your higher management with your intention to make up the cost differential later, use that account as a reference, or simply as a ploy to deny your competition the ability to secure that particular account.

Financial Stability. The initiation of the sale may take place but will the culmination happen? That is, will you get paid? Will all the checks clear? Good business requires that you make sure your prospect can afford to implement your solution. You must know if they are financially sound or not. Have they had a downturn in business? Can they meet their obligations? Financial criteria of this sort must be reviewed early in sales cycle to determine if this is, indeed, good business. Not-so-pleasant, after-the-fact surprises can negatively affect you and may even cost you your job. As a responsible professional, the results of your sales — good, bad or indifferent — rest squarely on your shoulders.

Technical Details. If this is a technical sale, review your final solution or response with your technical staff. Be certain that what you have proposed meets or exceeds all necessary specifications.

Make sure to review your response versus that of your competitors. Objectively discuss what it would take to have the best possible solution, one that is very attractive and well received by your client.

No Hidden Surprises. One of the worst sales that can happen is one which contains a hidden surprise. To avoid that happening, ask your internal coach, your unofficial representative inside the account, for objective feedback to help you become aware of any new or unknown circumstances that can undermine your sale.

The ability to ferret out this internal, unknown information is precisely why the development and continual engagement of an inside/internal coach is such an essential activity. By obtaining the inside scoop, your sales team can make any necessary adjustments to close this sale.

Once you and your company have determined that your pending sale is good business, it remains for you, the sales professional, to prepare and print copies of the binding contracts your company requires and review them to ensure all information is accurate and in order.

NOTES

chapter twenty-two

Closing the Deal

Most people have difficulty asking the important closing questions of life:

- Will you go out with me?
- Will you marry me?
- Will you hire me?

Why should it be any different when it comes to sales?

After many years in sales, I can answer that unfortunately it isn't any different. The greatest fear of many sales professionals is closing the deal.

The hardest thing to do is to ask for the sale:

- Can I sign you up?
- Will you buy?

It is not that I find it difficult to ask those uncomfortable questions, which, by the way are very necessary to ask. It is more amazing why many of us have such trepidations about asking for something that we have earned the right to ask for. More importantly, if someone truly wants what you have to offer, do you think for a minute that they would not be delighted you posed such a question?

Of course, you know the answer: closing is the formal response to a job well done. If you performed the job well, the close can be automatic and uneventful. Really, there will be no drama. And remember, when this technique of closing begins to take place, all those objections from the previous chapters begin to bubble up to the surface. But for our purposes, let's review the art of closing, which can simply be viewed as building up the nerve to ask the telling question or questions.

People buy from other people. No matter how elevated or philosophical you want to make it, sales is the simplest form of interpersonal exchange. Read the personality of your client. Understand them as an individual. Recognize that the culture of their company is unique. Keep all these circumstances in the forefront of your mind. Some people can be easily offended if your approach to closing seems too aggressive or even too lax.

Be confident! Look this person directly in the eyes and go for it! After all the effort and work you have demonstrated up to this point, you deserve the right to showcase yourself, similarly to a lawyer defending the client they believe is innocent.

I always prefer to close one-on-one, but there will be occasions when you may be closing in front of an entire group. Let them all talk when the closing situation occurs. It may seem uncomfortable, but as a solid sales professional, it is your job to lead them down the road of closure. You will guide that process by constantly gaining and asking for agreement. By this process, the final 'yes' is really a series of many smaller 'yeses' that chain together for a positive outcome.

Remember
- Bring any important documentation as material proof to support your closing efforts
- Always expect the unexpected
- Be prepared for everything
- It's too late to wish that you had some certain material that could have won an opportunity after the fact.

SALES CLOSES

The summary. This is the easiest and most utilized of all closes. Simply summarize all the main points that are favorable and gain agreement as you go along on the criteria you know are important to the decision-maker. At the conclusion of the conversation, ask for the order.

> "Mr. O'Connor you indicated that rapid response to Internet access was important to you. My new product allows the fastest Internet access time available today. That is an important aspect in your decision-making process, isn't it? And you said you agreed our system would improve your results, didn't you? Why don't we get you signed up right now so you can take immediate advantage of (our product)?"

Let's review the balance sheet. This is the second most common close. This close is similar to the Ben Franklin style of comparison, wherein you create two columns: one displaying the strengths of your solution, one pointing out your competition's weaknesses. Be certain that your proposed solution has many identifiable advantages when compared to your competition.

Third party referral. This close is added to another close. A good business referral from a respected source that can testify that your solution is "bullet-proof" can add tremendous value and credibility. If such a reference does exist, absolutely add that name to your closing comments with your prospective client.

I'll let you know. This closing type is in response to a decision-maker's attempt to postpone authorizing your sale. Decision-makers who 'sit on the fence' may require a little prodding. Before they can put you off, attempt to surface their objections.

> "I'm sure you have some issues you want to think over. Do you mind if I ask what they are?"
> Keep asking them a form of this question until you can say to them, "Have I answered all your objections?"

Last objection. This close is not the norm, but does surface every so often. This close occurs when all objections have been satisfied and are no longer in the forefront of your prospect's mind but he still does not want to sign the agreement. Obviously there is still something holding him back, so he might be swayed in this manner:

> "Mr. O'Connor, obviously I have not answered all of your concerns. Would you mind sharing the last remaining concern that's holding you back?"

Remember, you have earned the right to ask these questions! You cannot close a deal unless all objections have been surfaced.

Alternative solution. This close offers a potential customer a chance to make a decision immediately. By offering a choice, you may be able to get a commitment and complete the close.

> "Mr. O'Connor, would you like a red or blue model? What's your preference?"
> — or —
> "Solution 'A' is the more expensive decision. Wouldn't Solution 'B' still fit your needs, but at a lower cost to you?"

Fill in the order. This close assumes the sale. Fill out the order form and hand it to your prospect, along with your pen.

Alternative request. In this close, ask a presumptuous question or permission.

> "Mr. O'Connor, would you want this solution implemented on Wednesday or Friday of next week?"
> — or —
> "Is Jennie the person responsible for reordering your necessary supplies?"

Calling his hand. Although this sounds like a card game, all you are doing is bringing the process to a head.

"Mr. O'Connor, haven't you belabored this decision far too long? Isn't this decision getting dragged out so long that you are forced to continue to have to deal with a slow and outdated network? Why don't you just make the logical decision and sign this order right now?"

Surprisingly, sometimes such a closing technique brings a laugh to your prospect and a subsequent signing. However, know your prospect well before trying this!

Lost cause. In this close, the salesperson takes the hit. This is almost always a last-ditch effort to save a lost sale and almost never works. But if you are already out the door, what do you have to lose?

"Obviously, I have not done my job very well. I understand why you would not want to buy from me at this time. I only wish I had handled things differently. Can you reconsider your decision?"

What have been presented are techniques that can be used to close a sale. Knowing which close or closes to use, and when to use them, is not a science but an art. Closing, like all art, gets better and better the more you practice it. There is never any right way or wrong way to proceed. The better you know your clients, the more likely you are to choose the close that will work best with them at that time. Every close is a trial close – until it works. Signed orders represent closes that worked.

One of the consistent messages of this book is: Always Be Closing, which means that when presenting your final proposal, always request authorization of your solution. This can be a purchase order, a letter of intent, a signed order form, or even a verbal approval of intent to sign. To be successful at sales, always close.

The worst that can happen is a no.

The best that can happen is a yes!

ALWAYS BE CLOSING!

NOTES

chapter twenty-three

Staging the Final Contract

The last phase of the sale is staging the final contract. Sometimes when selling a complex, large-dollar solution, this process can be long and cumbersome.

Once an organization has made the decision to buy your solution, rarely does that organization change its mind. But this final step can cause great discomfort and unsettle your stomach, should both legal departments not be reasonably flexible.

Usually when a sales organization presents a final contract involving large revenues and great responsibilities, there is almost always a huge amount of fine print in the agreement for the legal protection of both parties. The customer is well aware of this and normally sends that contract to their team of corporate lawyers for their review and blessing. Your customer must always be aware of his or her job security, so such a step is necessary so that he will not lose face with the powers that be.

Your customer is almost as anxious as you are to get this legal step concluded but it's always a good idea to keep pressure on the process so it doesn't bog down and die from boredom.

To keep you on top of the process, ask your client's legal department to review your company's documents and recommend any perceived changes or modifications. Then forward those modifications to your company's legal department for review and approval.

For any lawyer reading this chapter, please don't take any of this personally, but some lawyers have been known to try to prove their worth by recommending changes just to recommend them and by disagreeing with your legal department's counter changes. Many of us have experience in some legal matter (for instance divorce), wherein both sides (your spouse and your lawyer) seem to take their time in reaching certain legal conclusions. I think that stems from getting paid by the hour rather than by the speedy completion of the project, but that's only a guess on my part!

If you seem to be involved in a situation like that, intervene. To solve these problems, both parties must engage in conversation; but to reach a speedy conclusion, they will need a mediator: you! I have been involved in sales with both legal departments discussing the issues. Do not become the legal departments' go between. Most sales professionals are not lawyers; let the legal professionals earn their money. Your job as mediator is to keep them on time, help them engage in direct conversations with each other, see that they address the real issues, and ensure that the sale takes place.

If things start to break down, bring your management into this process quickly. Never lose a sale because of faulty contract negotiations. Stay involved until both legal departments reach a mutual compromise. It is your job to salvage the final contract in any and all situations.

Once both legal departments have approved the changes and they have been incorporated into your final contract draft, your customer should show no hesitation in signing the final contract. Make sure you have read and fully understand any and all fine print. Although your prospect's legal department has approved the document, your direct client may still have some questions. Be prepared to answer any of his concerns.

Lastly, establish contingency planning by assigning specialized employees from your company whose job it is to see to the completion of the project. Your customer will also assign employees from his company to work with your people. Together, both your customer and you agree to begin and complete assigned tasks on specific dates.

By having both employees from your customer's company plus your company employees working on this project, there is less chance for failure.

chapter twenty-four

Implementing the Sale

Your sale may be completed but you are far from done. Not only are you responsible for seeing that an order is given and taken — and that the appropriate papers are signed and delivered — but as a top-notch sales professional you will be involved in making sure that the solution you have just sold is delivered correctly as well.

As the sale proceeds from the signing to the delivery, there is often a hand-off of activities to your organization's engineering and/ or project management team, especially when the sale involves technology, chemicals, or simply is very complicated and detail laden. Although your responsibilities officially may end once the selling is done, I strongly urge that you coordinate constantly with your delivery team so they don't drop the ball. What you are trying to avoid is a non-functional solution which would allow the customer to cancel your order.

As we all know, anything can go wrong at any given time; and if it does, the most unpleasant turn of events for you might be a commission charge-back. Definitely an unpleasant surprise you don't want to experience at any time, much less after having done so much hard work.

PROCEDURES THAT WILL KEEP YOU ON TRACK

First. Schedule an internal implementation-planning meeting shortly after the client has signed the contracts.

> • Don't wait for this process to automatically occur. Most companies have many sales people and if you don't shepherd your hard-earned deal personally, it could get stuck in some corporate pigeonhole.

> • Never trust this response:
> "Don't worry. Your sale is assigned to the Engineering Group. It's in the queue."

> If you put all your faith in statements like that, you are sure to be in for a huge surprise — and tons of worry.

Second. Insist on a project plan for this account from both engineering and project management that contains the exact completion dates for each and every element of the contract. (In most organizations, there is some version of engineering, project management, or the installation/field service group.)

Third. You may want to meet face-to-face with your client and your delivery team. While your contract probably contains a Statement of Work (SOW) — a legally binding document that clearly states the exact deliverables, the dates, and the price — it's always a good idea to verbally go over with the client exactly what your organization will be delivering and when that end result will be implemented.

In support of this meeting, your project manager may design an Implementation Schedule backed up by a Bill of Materials (a composite of all necessary products to be included with your solution). See that these documents get to the client and that both of you follow them as the process continues.

Fourth. Schedule regular status meetings to ensure that all of your client's objectives are being satisfied and that your Project Manager completes all necessary tasks.

TO BE SUCCESSFUL, EVERY PROJECT, REGARDLESS OF SIZE OR DOLLAR VALUE, MUST:

- Be completed on time
- Stay within the budgeted dollar amount specified in your contract
- Satisfy your customer's requirements 100%.

If these three are present:

- You will receive a favorable reference from the client.

If you fall short on ANY of these three:

- The unfavorable reference you might receive could severely taint, or even destroy, both your company and your personal business credibility.
- You will get no second chances, no free passes. This is a scenario without forgiveness;
- Both your current clients and your future clients will know. One poorly executed solution and people talk — and bad news travels fast.
- Bad references will negatively impact your ability to sell in the future and severely limit your effectiveness as a sales professional.

To prevent a poorly executed solution from harming you:

- Make sure your delivery team is accountable.
- Remember that no sale is ever too small to be ignored.
- Stay involved in the process until your solution is installed or completed and nothing more needs to be accomplished or provided by you and your company.
- Consistently and comprehensively inquire about the status of the project for your new client from your delivery team and/or higher management. Believe me, everyone involved will respect you for being thorough.

No one can sell or track your deal better than you!

NOTES

chapter twenty-five

Account Review and Recap

One of the most-often-ignored step in any process — and sales is no exception — is the review, or recap. While it might seem to be optional and non-essential, done correctly the review can generate more sales, revenue, efficiency, and effectiveness in the future. And review costs nothing but a little bit of your time. It's my experience that this is time extremely well spent.

After the sales process is complete, after you have celebrated, after you have spent your money or invested it, take a few minutes to interview your sales team to determine what was successful and what worked when selling this client. Once you know all the things you want to do more of, talk about what didn't work as well as you had hoped. These are things you want to do less of and/or modify before you do them again. The review process can uncover valuable information about selling future clients. Additionally, your organization can recognize what types of sales support works in assisting you with the sales process and what does not. Your company may, for example, determine that new skill development is necessary for the entire sales team. They may even want to change their processes and/or add new support personnel.

It is advisable to have a review session with your client as well. Discover why he bought from you and not from your competitor.

Find out from his or her perspective what was or was not successful in the sales process. Don't be concerned that they will not want to talk to you about this; usually, they will. I have noticed in my sales career a great willingness by my clients to share this kind of information in a very honest and open manner.

The review is the appropriate time to ask your client for referral business. Does your client know of anyone else who could utilize your products and/or service? If you have done everything suggested in this book, your new client will be only too happy to offer his personal referrals to you. Why? Because you have completely focused your attention on his or her requirements. Because you have maintained a totally professional attitude. And because you have provided a solution to his/her problems; a solution you made sure worked.

chapter twenty-six

Good Work Habits for
Selling in the Real World

Becoming a top-notch sales professional is not easy, but with hard work, determination, and a will to succeed, it can be done. Staying at the top of your game isn't easy, either. But with constant review and a willingness to learn and improve, it too, can be done.

As with all projects, review is the key to continued and future success. You should start by daily reviewing your successes. Too often, people seem to focus on their failures, on the things that didn't go right. The concept to keep in mind here is something called The Weightlifter's Law which says: That which you focus on gets stronger. If a bodybuilder is trying to improve his biceps, he doesn't do squats, he does curls. Likewise in life, that which we focus on gets stronger. If you start thinking about, and focusing on, the things that didn't go right, you will find yourself becoming negative and defeatist; you may know all the ways that something doesn't work but you will not have learned how to improve your game.

Instead, start by reviewing those things which did work. Analyze them and determine how you can do more. Then decide what you can do to make what worked even better. The key here is to know your strengths and make them stronger. Surprisingly, along the way your weaknesses will also improve.

To be a successful sales professional, you will have to focus on your strengths but don't ignore your weaknesses. If you spend your time trying to improve only your weaknesses, you will, if successful at that goal, simply become average all around. Trying to improve your weaknesses makes as much sense as trying to teach Babe Ruth to bunt or steal bases. Babe Ruth's strength was in hitting home runs. All his efforts were — and should have been — put into doing that better and more often.

If you put the same effort into improving your strengths instead of your weaknesses, you will eventually become an excellent sales professional. To improve those areas in which you are not as strong, hire assistants or partner with colleagues who are.

THE NEXT PART OF THE PROCESS:
REVIEW ON A REGULAR BASIS.

Review should happen daily, weekly, monthly, quarterly, and yearly. Each time frame has its own area for consideration.

DAILY. Look at the elements or action steps of selling; how many calls did you make, who did you talk to, what did they say? And so forth. Then look at what you weren't able to get done and reschedule it.

WEEKLY. At the end of every Friday, look at the overview of the week and modify your plans for the next week day by day, account by account.

MONTHLY. Assess your completions and achievements. Then compare them to your projections. Make adjustments, modify your plan, and put the new actions steps into your planning system.

QUARTERLY. Look at your successes from a longer-term basis, modify, and re-implement.

YEARLY. At the end of the year, assess your successes, determine what you'd like to achieve during the next year, and create your quarterly and monthly plans based on that.

Make sure you enter the action step elements into your planner on specific dates at specific times. If review is the key to success, writing down your conclusions and new action plans is the act required to turn your ideas into results.

In addition to reviewing the elements of your sales plans, you will also want to review and assess your attitude and work behaviors. I recommend doing that on a daily basis as sort of the motivator to get you moving in the morning. Here is the list I use. You may want to add other questions you find that you need to keep in mind.

The sales executive's daily mental check list:

- Am I being conscientious?
- Is my mental approach positive?
- Do I begin work early?
- Do I work a full day?
- Do I take too much time off?
- Do I waste time?
- Do I make enough sales calls?
- Do I have qualified prospects?
- Do I plan sales presentations properly?
- Do I deserve to close?
- Am I effective on sales calls?
- Do I review and plan on the weekend?
- Do I keep my sales materials and data organized?
- Do I maintain accurate records?
- Do I enjoy selling?

Becoming a sales professional and maintaining your level of competence takes work, hard work. But the results and the life you can create for yourself are worth every ounce of effort you put into it.

Success rarely comes without effort. And that which does is not as sweet as the success you create for yourself.

Sales is a great life. Enjoy it.

NOTES

conclusion

The Reality of Selling in the Real World

You are only as good as your last deal — which seems like a real slap in the face for someone who has diligently gone through the sales process outlined in this book. Unfortunately, that reality comes with the territory.

Here are a few tricks I use to keep it fresh:

> **Make it fun**. Enjoy what you do. Find the pleasure in every element, even when things don't turn out like you'd like them to.
>
> **Manage the pressure.** Don't let the pressure manage you. If you let things overwhelm you, you will most likely be driven from a career in sales.
>
> **Be inventive.** Try to revamp your approaches. Find what works and make it better. Find what doesn't work and make it different.
>
> **Redesign what you say.** Don't get into a verbal rut. If certain phrases always seem to work, keep them in your patter but find different ways to approach those phrases. If you get bored with what you say, your customers will sense it and your sales will plummet.

Create new pricing modules. Include more service for the same cost. Make your product/service/deliverables better and better.

Differentiate yourself. Make the customer see the difference you provide. Stand out from the crowd. Do it better. It may buy you new customers.

Be good to yourself. Don't beat up on yourself.

Be expectant. Expect to succeed, expect to make the sale, expect to win. Henry Ford said:

> "Whether you think you can do a thing or you think you can't do a thing, you're right."

If you think you can, you will. If you think you can't, you won't.

Always make your work fun. If work is no longer fun, change the way you're doing what you do or change what you're doing. If life and work aren't fun, they aren't worth doing.

Sales should be fun. Enjoy it.

the author

Larry Sternlieb was born to Dr. Max & Attorney Mollie Atleson Sternlieb into a family that valued hard work and self-determination.

Larry's father was the County Health Commissioner in Portage County, Ohio, for more than twenty years and is best known for ensuring that the children of Portage County, regardless of income, received The Salk Vaccine in the earliest days of the Polio Epidemic of the 1950s.

Mollie, Larry's mother, was the first woman graduate of the Akron University Law School and worked in the legal profession before retiring to raise her son.

When Larry was 9 years old, his father had a disabling stroke which paralyzed his left side. Throughout the next 10 years, Larry and his mother took care of his father. During that time, Larry's mother was diagnosed with cancer. Larry took care of both his parents until his father's death in January, 1971 and his mother's death the following May. After the death of his parents in his freshman year at Kent State University, Larry found himself entirely on his own with very little money.

To pay his way through college, Larry taught college classes, worked construction during summers, and earned a graduate assistantship for his Master's Degree. He served in the Student Senate for two years, speaking at various functions on behalf of the Student Body and the University. He was featured in numerous articles for the student newspaper, and developed an energy workshop focused on saving natural resources and money. He was also coordinator for the Committee on Political Education (COPE) organizing voter registration drives and introducing national speakers at the university.

Following graduation from Kent State University (with two Bachelor's Degrees and a Master's Degree), Larry went into sales where he applied the same intensity and effort that got him successfully through college. His first sales position was with one of America's leading sales organizations, Xerox.

His first year with Xerox saw Larry honored as Rookie of the Year. The next two years he led the branch in sales and was awarded Top Sales Rep/Marketing Rep of the Year for Northern Ohio. His career in sales is filled with successes from high profile companies like Trend Micro, Citrix Systems, General Electric Consulting Corporation, General Data Comm, Black Box, McDonnell Douglas, and Prime Computer. He has served as both sales manager and sales executive, regularly obtaining Pro and President Club status while consistently exceeding his quota.

Having been trained in virtually all of the best sales training programs, Larry decided it was time to apply his training and experience in a manner that would help other sales personnel and potential sales personnel achieve the success and enjoyment he has experienced in more than forty years of sales. From that desire, Larry created Larry Sternlieb Seminars (LSS, LLC), a sales training methodology based on his personal experiences and practices. LSS training is unique in that it uses only 'real world' practices geared for the technology and rapid pace of the Twenty-First Century.

LSS offers both seminars to individual companies to train their staff and as well options for individual sales personnel and smaller organizations to take advantage of.

For more information, contact Larry@sellingintherealworld. com and visit the website www.sellingintherealworld.com

acknowledgments

I wish to thank my editor, Randy Martin; Morgan James founder, David Hancock; publisher, Jim Howard; and author relations manager, Emily Madison.

bibliography

"Unlimited Power" Anthony Robbins, Balantine Books, 1986

"See You at the Top" Zig Ziglar, Zig Ziglar Corporation, 1977

"Think and Grow Rich" Napoleon Hill, Wellshire Book Company, 1966

"How to Become a Rainmaker" Jeffrey Fox, Hyperion Co., 2000

"The One Minute Manager," Kenneth Blanchard, Berkley Books, 1981

"Asking Questions" Stephen Schiffman, DEI Management Group, 1996

"The Magic of Thinking Big," David J. Schwartz, Simon and Schuster, 1981

"Fish!" Stephen Lundin, Ph.D, Harry Paul, John Christiensen, Many Rivers Press, 2000

"Purple Cow," Seth Godin, Penguin Publishing Group, 2009

"Strengths Finder 2.0," Tom Rath, Gallup Press, 2007

"Who Moved My Cheese?" Spencer Johnson, MD, J. P. Putnam Sons, NY, 1998

"Strategic Selling," Robert Miller, Stephen Heiman, William Morrow & Company, 1985

"The Art of War," Sun Tzu, Dell Publishing, 1983

"Xerox Telephonics," Xerox Corporation Manual,1979

"Leasing and Consulting," Amembal Isom, General Electric Manual, 1986

"Vanguard," Holden Corporation Manual, 1984

"Creative Visualization," Shatki Gawain, The New World Library, 1982

"Target Account Selling," Valkyrie Management Company, 1984

"The Versatile Salesperson," Wilson Learning Company, 1985

"Productivity Skills," Spectrum Training Corporation, 1981

"Solution Selling," Keane Incorporated, 1993

"Selling from the Customer's Viewpoint," General Electric Company, Parad IGM Group, Inc, 1991

"Executive Selling Program," General Electric Consulting Services, Kappa Group, 1987

"Xerox Interpersonal Selling Strategies," Xerox Learning Systems, 1985

"In Search of Excellence," Thomas J. Peters, Robert Waterman, Jr., Harper and Row Publishers, 1984

"Selling to Vito," Anthony Parinello, Adams Media Corporation, 1999

"Power Based Selling," Holden Corporation, 1986

"The Phoenix Project," Gene Kim, Kevin Behr, George Spaford, IT Revolution Press, 2018

"The Erroneous Zone," Dr. Wayne Dyer, Funk & Wagnalls, 1976

"How to Win Friends and Influence People," Dale Carnegie, Simon and Schuster, 1936

"Question Based Selling," Thomas A. Freese, Sourcebooks, 2013

"Love is Letting Go of Fear," Gerald Jampolsky, MD, Celestial Arts, 1979

Technical Sales Training Programs and Manuals from Trend Micro

Technical Sales Training Programs and Manuals from Citrix

index

A free ebook edition is available with the purchase of this book.

To claim your free ebook edition:

1. Visit MorganJamesBOGO.com
2. Sign your name CLEARLY in the space
3. Complete the form and submit a photo of the entire copyright page
4. You or your friend can download the ebook to your preferred device

Morgan James
BOGO™

A **FREE** ebook edition is available for you
or a friend with the purchase of this print book.

CLEARLY SIGN YOUR NAME ABOVE

Instructions to claim your free ebook edition:
1. Visit MorganJamesBOGO.com
2. Sign your name CLEARLY in the space above
3. Complete the form and submit a photo
   of this entire page
4. You or your friend can download the ebook
   to your preferred device

Print & Digital Together Forever.

Snap a photo

Free ebook

Read anywhere

CPSIA information can be obtained
at www.ICGtesting.com
Printed in the USA
JSHW082053120723
44647JS00002B/3

9 781636 980768